Reminiscences
— of an —
Octogenarian

Reminiscences
— of an —
Octogenarian

BRUCE MANNING METZGER

HENDRICKSON
PUBLISHERS

© 1997 by Hendrickson Publishers, Inc.
P. O. Box 3473
Peabody, Massachusetts 01961–3473
Printed in the United States of America

ISBN 1–56563–264–8

First Printing — October 1997

Library of Congress Cataloging-in-Publication Data

Metzger, Bruce Manning.
    Reminiscences of an octogenarian / Bruce M. Metzger
    Includes bibliographical references and index.
    ISBN 1–56563–264–8 (cloth: alk. paper)
    1. Metzger, Bruce Manning. 2. New Testament
scholars—United States—Biography. 3. Biblical
scholars—United States—Biography. I. Title.
BS2351.M48A3 1997
220'.092—dc21
[B]   97–28490
                                                                    CIP

This book is printed on acid-free paper.

To Isobel

My wife and best friend,
whose consistent Christian life and love
have guided, inspired, and sustained me

~·

TABLE OF CONTENTS

LIST OF ILLUSTRATIONS

PREFACE

IT has often been remarked that the snare of autobiographers is that we see ourselves neither as others see us nor as God sees us. We are tempted to concentrate on a few particulars of our life, and to make these selections—chosen to exhibit ourselves at our best—representative of the whole. The result is not really honest, for no one is a good critic of his or her own career.

What then can be done? It is possible, I think, and may be useful, to present memoirs of a life which, from its length, is a connecting link with events in the past, often forgotten and sometimes misrepresented.

Set within a generally chronological framework, the following chapters describe several long-range projects in which I had a share in the organization, ongoing activities, and final product. Over the years these involved such tasks as editing *The Greek New Testament,* translating the Bible, condensing it for *The Reader's Digest Bible,* and assembling several volumes, such as *The Oxford Companion to the Bible.* Other less ambitious undertakings are also recorded, along with occasional mishaps and recurring vexations. While drawing up the chapters I have tried to bear in mind Voltaire's sage comment, "The surest way to be boring is in striving to be exhaustive."

It is unfortunate that the pronoun "I" occurs with some frequency. But it could hardly be otherwise, since it is my own reminiscences and not someone else's that are being recorded.

MY PENNSYLVANIA DUTCH HERITAGE

THE rolling hills of Lancaster County, Pennsylvania, and portions of adjacent counties, including Dauphin, Lebanon, and Berks, are dotted with prosperous and well-kept farms. Those who originally developed these homesteads had responded to William Penn's invitation to settle in the New World. They came from areas along the Rhine, and from Alsace, Bavaria, and German Switzerland. Between 1727 and 1775 some sixty-eight thousand newcomers arrived.

The English whom they met when they got off the ship at Philadelphia ridiculed their outlandish dialect and their preposterous customs. Writers and historians have marveled over the tenacity with which these people we now call the Pennsylvania Dutch[1] have clung to their language and their customs. The Quakers, already secure in their political and economic domination of the state, soon found this great tide of immigration threatening and formidable. By the time of the American Revolution, the population of Pennsylvania, according to Benjamin Franklin, was one-third German.

Among the Pennsylvania Dutch were several different religious groups. The largest number were Lutheran and Reformed in their church affiliation. Others belonged to one or another group of Anabaptists, a comprehensive modern

---

[1]"Dutch" is an anglicized form of *Deutsch* (meaning "German") and has nothing to do with Holland Dutch.

designation of those who denounced the baptism of infants and insisted that only adult baptism of believers was valid. This so-called left wing of the Reformation, firmly opposed to formalism and ritual in religion, had been severely persecuted in Europe by Roman Catholics and Protestants alike. Those put to death probably exceeded ten thousand.

The earliest Anabaptists to come to America were Mennonites, followers of Menno Simons. They stressed the idea of the community of believers (with no marriage outside the community) and required extreme plainness of dress, avoidance of legal oaths and military service, and simplicity of church organization (clergy received no salary). Large numbers of Mennonites settled in Lancaster County, where today they own the greatest part of this rich farmland, one of the most fertile and productive counties in the United States.

The Amish, whose extreme peculiarities of dress and custom set them apart, followed Jacob Amman and broke from the Mennonite Church because they were convinced that even more strictness should be observed in their everyday life. The "Hook and Eye Amish," for example, wear no buttons on their clothes, for in the old days buttons were the insignia of the military. The "House Amish" have no church buildings but worship in the houses or barns of members of the congregation. "Old Order Amish" ride only in buggies or wagons and have no telephones, electricity, or other modern conveniences in their homes.

Not all of the German immigrants were farmers. There were ministers, scholars, physicians, scientists; there were carpenters, weavers, potters, blacksmiths, printers, stone-cutters, saddlers, and butchers (a German word for "butcher" is *Metzger*). Many of those who had trades farmed as well, carrying on their crafts in the spare time that farming left them, especially during the winter season. Most of them kept their individual dialect because it was for them the most expressive way of saying something. Remnants of these dialects still persist. Those who still use Pennsylvania Dutch in Berks County refer to potatoes as *Gardoffeln* (from

High German *Kartoffeln*), whereas in Lancaster County potatoes are called *Grumbiere* (from Low German *Grundbirne*, meaning "ground pears").

More than eighty years ago I was born on February 9, 1914, at Middletown, in Dauphin County, Pennsylvania. This town of about six thousand inhabitants is located on the Susquehanna River ten miles southeast of Harrisburg, the capital of the state. It had gained its name during stagecoach days, for it was the midpoint between Lancaster and Carlisle, and the horses were changed there. I was the first of two children of Maurice R. Metzger (1884–1980) and Anna Manning Metzger (1889–1985). According to my father's investigation of genealogical records, the American branch of his family began in the middle of the eighteenth century when his great-great-grandfather, Jacob Metzger, a resident of the Rhine Valley where it enters Holland, came to the United States. Here he settled on a tract of land that came to be known as "Metzger's Choice" in Lancaster County, a few miles south of Middletown, bordering the Susquehanna River. He and his immediate descendants were farmers by occupation and Mennonites by conviction. As members of a "peace church," and with memories of religious persecution in Europe, they were opposed to warfare and did not participate in the War for Independence.

George Manning, my mother's great-grandfather, had come from England toward the end of the eighteenth century. A shipbuilder in his own country, he seems to have become a farmer in his new homeland. Here he and his descendants intermarried with Pennsylvania German settlers in Lancaster County.

My father's early schooling was in a one-room country schoolhouse. Not satisfied with having completed the prescribed eight grades of study there, he wished to pursue further education. Consequently, in addition to assisting his parents with chores on the farm, he walked or rode his bicycle three miles to Middletown in order to attend the high school there. He would study Latin grammar

Maurice R. Metzger

while plowing—having burned a hole with a red-hot poker through the margin of the book so it could be tied to the cross-beam of the plow. In 1903 he was graduated as valedictorian of his class, but for some reason his parents did not attend the graduation ceremony. After two years of teaching in a newly established one-room country school not far from where had begun his own schooling, he enrolled in Lebanon Valley College; by accelerating

Anna Manning Metzger

his studies, he was graduated with the Bachelor of Arts degree in 1907. Following a year of teaching Latin and German in the Middletown High School, he attended the Law School of the University of Pennsylvania. In 1911 he was admitted to the Dauphin County Bar Association, and the following year he became a member of the Harrisburg firm of Wickersham & Metzger, in which association he continued until 1920 when his partner was appointed judge.

In 1924 he formed a partnership with F. Brewster Wickersham, a son of his former partner.

For fifty-five years my father practiced law, going by train in the morning, six days a week, to his office in Harrisburg, and in evenings seeing clients in his office at our home in Middletown. Besides his law practice, he also was elected to serve for two terms as a Republican representative of Dauphin County in the Pennsylvania state legislature.

As a child I was rather frail and subject to respiratory troubles. An operation for appendicitis when I was six years old was followed by a long period of recuperation. During the rest of that year my mother taught me at home. Some years later, and partly to encourage me to be involved in out-of-doors physical exercise, my father arranged for part of the garden lying beyond the garage to be made into a tennis court. He and I dug the holes for the poles, and a local carpenter put up the wire netting. Although the court was a few feet short of regulation length, it was a popular gathering place for young people of the age of my sister Edith and myself.

Besides tennis my hobbies included making ship models of various sizes as well as one-tube, battery-operated radio sets. As a novelty, I built a radio set inside a quart jar; the variable condenser for tuning the set was made from metal I cut from a tin can. Another project on which I spent hours and hours was putting together a ship model inside a bottle, the neck of which was too narrow to allow the passage of a five-cent piece. Much easier was the production of a similar curiosity when, one springtime, I inserted the blossom of a gourd plant in our garden into the neck of a Listerine bottle and allowed nature to take its course.

After Charles Lindberg made his solo flight across the Atlantic in May of 1927 I constructed a wooden model of his airplane, the *Spirit of St. Louis*. For some weeks the three-foot-long replica hung on display in the window of Raymond's Hardware Store in the downtown business district of Middletown. During those years I also made several more useful objects, such as a large cedar chest and a banjo

Bruce, thirteen years old

clock case in which I installed an electric clock movement. The clock is still in use, hanging on the wall of our dining room at Princeton, and the chest is in the attic, containing woolen blankets and other materials.

It was, of course, natural that my father hoped to see on the shingle, as he put it, "Metzger and Son" as the title of his law firm. With this in mind, he suggested that I begin to read Sir William Blackstone's classic work, *Commentaries on the*

Laws of England. I was, however, more interested in the pure English style of the author than in the subject matter itself. Although my father was, I am sure, disappointed with my rather negative reaction to the volume, he generously commented that, inasmuch as he had not remained on the farm in accord with his father's wishes, he would not urge me to undertake a type of study in which I had no real interest.

After graduation in 1931 from Middletown High School, where I had followed the academic course of study involving four years of Latin, I set off for college, choosing my father's alma mater, Lebanon Valley College. First-year students were expected to enroll for a foreign language, and for some reason I chose the elementary course in classical Greek grammar. Perhaps my choice was based, to some extent, on my recollection of a remark that I had heard a visiting minister make one Sunday, to the effect that the meaning of the original Greek of the text for his sermon that morning was not fully brought out in translations commonly available. Although I am doubtful now whether he was entirely correct in his understanding of the Greek of that text (1 Peter 2:7), at any rate I had never before realized that the New Testament was written originally in Greek. In any case, having elected in my freshman year to study Greek, I developed a liking for the language, and the following year I decided to enroll for the second course, during which we reviewed the elements of White's classical Greek grammar that we had used the previous year and translated sections of Xenophon's *Anabasis.*

My professor of Greek, Gustavus A. Richie, had taken an M.A. degree under George A. Barton at the University of Pennsylvania. Included in his graduate work was the study of New Testament textual criticism. Consequently, during my third year of Greek, when we read part of the book of Acts in Greek, Richie introduced us to James Hardy Ropes's magisterial work, *The Text of Acts,*[2] and had

---

[2]Volume 3 of *The Beginnings of Christianity* (ed. F. J. Foakes Jackson and Kirsopp Lake; London: Macmillan, 1926).

us make a comparison of a section of the Greek text of Acts preserved in two divergent manuscripts, Codex Vaticanus and Codex Bezae. Observing my interest in the subject, he lent me his copy of A. T. Robertson's *Introduction to the Textual Criticism of the New Testament*,[3] as well as Westcott and Hort's volume 2,[4] where the principles of textual criticism are set forth in great detail—most of which I certainly did not comprehend at that time.

In reading Robertson's volume I noticed that one of the books he frequently quoted was E. Jacquier's *Texte du Nouveau Testament* (Paris, 1913). Since I had begun the study of French the previous year, I thought that with Jacquier's book I could extend my interest in textual criticism as well as diversify my reading in French during my second-year course in that language. A letter to Robertson at Louisville Baptist Theological Seminary brought information as to the name and address of the publisher in Paris, and I ordered a copy of Jacquier. In due time the volume arrived. The cost in 1934 for this book of 535 pages was the equivalent of forty cents—and for another forty cents I had it bound partly in leather! Since there was no index in the volume, I entered on the blank pages at the end of the volume the page references to several hundred New Testament passages about which the author had text-critical comments.

Besides taking a fourth year of Greek under Professor Richie, when we read several of the epistles in the New Testament, I was fortunate that the professor of Latin, Alvin H. M. Stonecipher, kindly agreed to offer two semesters of Greek. Stonecipher, who had taken his Ph.D. degree at Vanderbilt University with a dissertation on Graeco-Persian proper names, was interested in many things and proposed that during one semester we translate Plato's *Euthyphro,* and during the other semester several of the Apostolic Fathers. (I was the only student who enrolled for these courses.)

---

[3] Second ed.; London: Hodder & Stoughton, 1928.
[4] *The New Testament in the Original Greek, Introduction* [and] *Appendix* (New York: Harper & Brothers, 1882).

Using the *editio minor* of the *Patrum Apostolicorum Opera,* edited by Gebhardt, Harnack, and Zahn,[5] I thus became acquainted with the Greek text of the *Didache,* several epistles of Ignatius and of Polycarp, as well as the *Martyrdom of Polycarp.*

In addition to these courses in Greek, I had continued the study of Latin for three years and also enrolled for three years of German. Along with the usual courses in English literature, a semester's course on the history of the development of the English language caught my fancy. All in all, as I look back now, I feel that I was particularly fortunate in the scope and kinds of instruction made available on the campus of a small liberal arts college with an enrollment of about six hundred students. The quality of the instruction is perhaps indicated in the following. Before being graduated in the spring of 1935 I entered the competition Bimillennium Horatianum that had been organized among the fifty-some colleges and universities throughout Pennsylvania in order to commemorate the two-thousandth anniversary of the birth of the Roman poet Horace (65–8 BC). The competition involved submitting an original translation of Horace's famous *Carmen Saeculare,* written in celebration of the Secular Games held in 17 BC. For my metrical translation the judges awarded me third prize, a copy of Wickham's Oxford edition of selected odes of Horace.

Other forays that I made into the field of Latin literature involved translating and annotating passages in the writings of two pagan authors who had commented briefly on the early Christians. One was Tacitus's account in his *Annals* (15.44) concerning Nero's persecution of Christians following the great fire at Rome in AD 64. The other was Pliny the Younger's epistle (10.96) asking the emperor Trajan how he, as governor of Bithynia in AD 112, should deal with Christians who persisted in meeting together despite an imperial decree that forbad such gatherings.

---

[5]Editio sexta minor; Leipzig: J. C. Hinrichs, 1920.

The two articles were published in a monthly journal, *Christian Faith and Life,* now long defunct, issued at Reading, Pennsylvania.

During my last two years in college I had begun to buy various kinds of reference works that I needed then or thought I might need in the future. Among these were, of course, dictionaries of Latin, Greek, German, and French— all of them in the Follett Foreign Language Series. Early in my study of New Testament Greek I acquired a copy of J. H. Thayer's *Greek-English Lexicon of the New Testament.* Toward the close of my college career I happened to attend a public auction of household effects near the college campus and purchased a fine, leather-bound copy of an early edition of the unabridged Liddell-Scott *Greek-English Lexicon.*

Other purchases were made at a secondhand bookshop located in the countryside of Lancaster County near the village of Blue Ball. This enterprise was owned and operated by a Mennonite bishop named Weaver, who kept the books in his barn. On several trips there I was able to acquire at very reasonable prices such sets as the five volumes of James Hastings's *Dictionary of the Bible* and the four volumes of Henry Alford's *Greek Testament,* with its concise commentary and critical apparatus for the Greek text.[6] This last work, which badly needed rebinding, cost me only one dollar.

Toward the latter part of my college career I began to wonder how I could combine my interest in the Greek language with some kind of Christian vocation. When a friend suggested that perhaps I might become a teacher of New Testament Greek, I immediately recognized that this was the kind of work I would find altogether congenial. I therefore began to make plans to study at Louisville under A. T. Robertson, one of the leading New Testament scholars of the time. However, before actually making formal application for such a program of study I learned that Robertson had died in September of 1934. I therefore began

---

[6]New York: Scribner's, 1909–11; Boston: Lee & Shepard, 1881.

to consider other institutions, and ultimately decided upon Princeton Theological Seminary.

One of my student friends at Lebanon Valley College was K. Morgan Edwards, who later became a professor of preaching at Claremont, California. He had graduated one year before me and was currently enrolled in his first year of study at Princeton Seminary. Edwards was also serving as the pastor of a small Methodist congregation at Hummelstown, about five miles from Middletown. Every Monday he would drive to Princeton, returning to his parish on Friday evening. It was on November 12th of 1934, during my senior year at college, that I arranged to go with him to Princeton in order to visit the seminary campus and then to return by train that same day. While at the Seminary there was opportunity for an interview with the registrar, Edward Howell Roberts, to whom I mentioned my hope of preparing myself to teach New Testament Greek. In due course several months later, after having made application for admission, I was accepted as a student for entrance in the autumn of 1935.

The summer prior to beginning my studies at Princeton provided time for acquiring better facility with the touch system of typing—a skill that has proved useful over the years. My reading during that summer was diversified and included several books on the life and literature of ancient Greece and Rome, Matthew Arnold's *Literature and Dogma,* and B. H. Streeter's *The Four Gospels.*[7] The State Library at Harrisburg had several books about the debate occasioned by the publication of the (British) Revised Version of the New Testament of 1881, and I made the acquaintance of the critical assessments of the translation written by Dean Burgon, J. B. Lightfoot, R. C. Trench, and Bishop Ellicott. I also completed reading through the entire Bible for the twelfth time—a practice of consecutive reading that I had begun five or six years earlier.

---

[7]Boston: James R. Osgood, 1873; London: Macmillan, 1924.

Chapter 2

MOVING ON TO PRINCETON

IN colonial days four small villages, named Kingstown, Queenstown, Princetown, Princesstown, were located along a ten-mile stretch of the road running between Trenton and New Brunswick, New Jersey. In the course of time, Kingstown became Kingston; Princetown, which grew so as to incorporate within its boundaries what had been Queenstown, became Princeton; and Princesstown decreased in size and is represented today by only a small cemetery. It was to the developing community of Princeton that in 1756 the College of New Jersey was moved from northern New Jersey into the newly constructed Nassau Hall—said to be at that time the largest building in the colonies. The college, which later came to be called Princeton University, was originally established in 1746 in the home of the Reverend Jonathan Dickinson of Elizabethtown, partly in order to provide education for Presbyterian ministers in the colonies.

Early in the following century the General Assembly of the Presbyterian Church debated the wisdom of establishing a theological seminary so as to make available further training for ministerial candidates who had completed four years of liberal arts study. Eventually, in 1811, the assembly authorized the establishment of a seminary and drew up a detailed "Plan of the Theological Seminary." According to this plan, the purpose of the Seminary was

> to unite in those who shall sustain the ministerial office, religion and literature; that piety of heart, which is the fruit only of the renewing and sanctifying grace and God, with

solid learning; believing that religion without learning, or learning without religion, in the ministers of the gospel, must ultimately prove injurious to the Church.

The first professor was a learned and scholarly Virginian, Archibald Alexander, formerly president of Hampden-Sydney College and, since 1807, the pastor of the Third Presbyterian Church (Pine Street), Philadelphia, one of the largest congregations in the nation. In 1812 Alexander was entrusted by the General Assembly with the organization of Princeton Theological Seminary, which was associated with but separate from the College of New Jersey. Lectures began in August of that year with three students meeting for classes in Alexander's home. For the first year he taught all subjects, but as other professors were added he confined himself to pastoral and polemic theology.

By the spring of 1813, the student body had increased to nine, a number that placed a heavier burden on the solitary professor and began to strain the dormitory facilities available to seminary students in the College of New Jersey's Nassau Hall. Consequently, in the autumn of 1813 a second professor was appointed to the seminary faculty. This was Samuel Miller, who had previously published, among other books, a learned discussion in two volumes entitled *A Brief Retrospect of the Eighteenth Century*,[1] a comprehensive survey of philosophy, theology, science, and cultural history in general.

In 1814 the Board of Directors recommended that a building be constructed at Princeton to provide for all educational, religious, dining, and housing needs of the theological students. The building, similar in structure to Nassau Hall, was designed by John McComb, Jr., the architect of such buildings as the current City Hall of New York. In the following year the General Assembly made $15,000 available for the proposed building, which today is called Alexander Hall, and which, when completed in 1818, cost more than $47,000.

---

[1] New York: T. & J. Swords, 1803.

The third professor, who had completed his study at Princeton Seminary in 1819, was Charles Hodge. Following an additional year of reading and study, in 1820 Hodge was appointed as tutor at the Seminary in order to assist Alexander and Miller in coping with increasing student enrollment. He remained there for the rest of his life, except for two years' study in France and Germany (1826–28). Thus began the longest and most remarkable tenure of any professor at Princeton Theological Seminary, first as professor of Oriental and biblical literature (1822–40), then as professor of theology until his death in 1878.

Such was the beginning of Princeton Theological Seminary, to which the writer of these memoirs came as a student in the autumn of 1935. The Seminary had grown over the years, and eighty-five other students enrolled with me in the class of 1938. Three separate dormitories and four eating clubs provided accommodations for a student body of some two hundred and fifty young men. There was no charge for tuition or room rent, but a fee of twenty-four dollars a year was assessed for light and heat. The charge for board in one of the four cooperative student clubs did not exceed six and a half dollars a week. Three years later the annual charge for room, light, and heat had risen to fifty dollars. The academic year covered thirty-four weeks, which included two weeks of Christmas vacation. Most of the courses for the Bachelor of Theology degree were prescribed; only about 7 percent of the total number of lecture hours during the three years were available for elective courses.

An examination was administered in the opening days of the first semester in order to ascertain a student's knowledge of the Greek language. Those who were judged to be lacking sufficient knowledge were required to take a four-hour course for one semester devoted to the review of Greek grammar; those who had never studied the language were required to enroll in a two-semester course of beginner's Greek. Because of my previous study of Greek I was able to begin the study of Hebrew my first year. After completing

the first semester under the patient tutelage of George Handy
Wailes (who, among other things, had us memorize the first
chapter of Genesis in Hebrew), I was transferred, with a
dozen or so other students, to a more advanced section
taught by a remarkable linguist, Henry Snyder Gehman.

At the University of Pennsylvania Gehman had earned
the Ph.D. in Indo-European philology; later he studied
Semitic languages and Egyptology at Dropsie College in
Philadelphia, and Hebrew and theology at the University of
Chicago Divinity School. He also earned the S.T.B. and
S.T.D. degrees in Old Testament and Semitic languages at
the Divinity School of the Protestant Episcopal Church in
Philadelphia. His teaching experience included German
and Spanish at South Philadelphia High School, and Latin
and Sanskrit at the University of Pennsylvania. An ordained minister of the Reformed Church, he had also
begun a mission church in north Philadelphia, where he
conducted services in German (1917–21).

In 1929 Dr. Gehman was invited to Princeton University as an instructor in Arabic and other Semitic languages.
A year later, because Dr. J. Gresham Machen had left the
Seminary in order to found Westminster Theological Seminary, Gehman was invited to teach New Testament Greek
in his place. In 1931, four years before I arrived in Princeton,
he was appointed professor of Old Testament literature at
the Seminary. In addition to Hebrew and Aramaic, he was
prepared to teach Syriac, Ethiopic, Armenian, and Coptic.

My professor in New Testament was William Park
Armstrong, a cultured Southerner born in Selma, Alabama.
A graduate of Princeton University and of Princeton Seminary, he had also studied at Marburg, Berlin, and Erlangen.
Armstrong combined exegetical skills with a critical appreciation of philosophical trends that had influenced the interpretation of the Scriptures. Unlike Dr. Gehman, who would
expend considerable energy in lecturing, often in a stento-
rian voice, Dr. Armstrong spoke rather softly and his words
did not always carry to the rear of the classroom. Students
who were keen not to miss anything of the lecture would

Professor William Park Armstrong

therefore sit in the front rows. Among Armstrong's manner-isms was his habit of making an occasional wry remark, at which he would raise his eyebrows and sniff once or twice.

Dr. Armstrong's required course in New Testament introduction and exegesis comprised lectures on (1) the language of the New Testament, its relation to antecedent and contemporary Greek, and its distinctive characteristics; (2) textual criticism according to the principles and the history of the text developed by Westcott and Hort; and (3) the canon, involving the fundamental idea, limiting prin-ciple, and process of organization in the first three centuries of the church. The lectures on exegesis followed the gram-matico-historical method, illustrated by a detailed study of the Greek text of the first eight chapters of the Epistle to the Romans.

Among my other first-year courses of what can be described as a classical curriculum in theology and church history was a lecture course on systematic theology under Caspar Wistar Hodge, Jr., the last of the Hodge dynasty at the Seminary. He died during the spring semester, and two of his students (G. Hall Todd and I) were invited to serve as pallbearers at the funeral service.

During my first year in Seminary I recall attending an interesting series of lectures on the books of the Apocrypha, given at the Trinity Episcopal Church, which is located across the street from the Seminary. On six Tuesday evenings the Reverend Canon Edgar Lewis Sanford came from Trinity Cathedral in Trenton and presented a general introduction to the Old Testament Apocrypha. Although during the summer between my first and second years in college I had read through the traditional King James Version of these books, my appreciation for such literature was considerably enlarged through the sympathetic orientation presented by someone for whom these books were of liturgical significance.

During my second year the prescribed courses included Hebrew exegesis under Dr. Gehman and Gospel history under Dr. Armstrong. This latter course surveyed literature on the life of Christ and evaluated the extent and character of the sources. The Gospel according to Mark and selections from the other Gospels were assigned in Greek. Likewise, students were expected to read about two dozen selections in Greek and Latin from Jewish and early Christian and Roman authors. These selections were made available in a booklet entitled *Texts for Gospel History,* privately printed in 1930 at Armstrong's expense at Princeton University Press. Those whose knowledge of Greek and Latin was insufficient to cope with the original text of the selections could purchase mimeographed copies of an English translation from an enterprising student of the senior class. Thus, at whatever level of linguistic attainment, Armstrong's students were exposed to a sound and basic methodology of examining, preferably in the original, the literary and historical sources from Josephus, Tacitus, Pliny, Clement of Alexandria, Origen, Eusebius, Jerome, and other patristic texts bearing on the date, composition, and authorship of the Gospels.

Following the death of the venerable Caspar Wistar Hodge, Jr., the Seminary invited Otto Piper to teach theology. Because Piper had taken a stand against Hitler, he was

Professors Henry S. Gehman and Otto A. Piper

no longer allowed to lecture in his homeland but had fled to Britain from Münster, where he had replaced Karl Barth as professor of theology. It goes without saying that Princeton students found a difference in style and presentation, as well as orientation, from previous lectures in systematic theology. Piper, who had studied under Hans Lietzmann in Germany and had taken his doctorate in ethics at Paris, had encyclopedic learning. Of him Emil Brunner said, perhaps with a tinge of sarcasm, "Piper knows everything." At any rate, the range of his knowledge was amazing, and he seemed to have a considered opinion on virtually every intellectual topic that was under discussion.

Besides enrolling in Piper's course in theology and other required courses, I elected to take biblical Aramaic under Gehman. This was a one-semester course in which we read the Aramaic portion of the book of Daniel. Naturally we made use of James A. Montgomery's commentary on that book in the International Critical Commentary series, to which volume Gehman had made valuable contributions.[2]

I also found time to audit several courses in classics at Princeton University on subjects that had been unavailable at Lebanon Valley College; these were courses on Herodotus, Euripides, and Greek patristics. In patristics, a graduate course, we read the Greek text of Justin Martyr's two apologies.

During my third year Dr. Armstrong lectured on apostolic history. This involved an introduction to Acts and the character of primitive Christian faith and its relation to the messianic work and the resurrection of Jesus. The Acts of the Apostles in Greek was assigned for study by students on their own, subject to examination. Questions concerning the chronology of the New Testament period had been one of Armstrong's earlier special interests, the fruits of which had been published in a concise and learned article in *The International Standard Bible Encyclopaedia*.[3]

My studies in Semitic languages continued under Gehman with an elective course on the Apocrypha and Pseudepigrapha, in which we translated portions of Israel Lévi's unpointed Hebrew text of Sirach. During the second semester we translated and sought to understand the first section of the prophecy of Ezekiel. For me, however, the most rewarding course was an entire year devoted to Syriac. After beginning with T. H. Robinson's *Paradigms and Exer-*

---

[2]*A Critical and Exegetical Commentary on the Book of Daniel* (ICC; New York: Scribner's, 1927).

[3]Chicago: Howard-Severance, 1915.

cises in Syriac Grammar,[4] Gehman had us continue with the *Chrestomathie* in Carl Brockelmann's *Syrische Grammatik,*[5] translating selections from the Peshitta, the *Teaching of Addai,* the *Chronicle of Edessa,* and some of the poetry of Ephraem.

Each year at the Seminary several prizes and fellowships were open for competition, based on papers written on pre-announced subjects. As it turned out, I was awarded a prize at the close of my first year and two other prizes at the close of my second year. The competition for a one-thousand dollar fellowship entailed a much more substantial paper. During my senior year the topic set for the paper was the exegesis of 1 Peter 3:13–22, which contains the enigmatic reference to Christ's going to preach to the spirits in prison. I decided early in my senior year to enter the competition and was fortunate enough at graduation in the spring of 1938 to be awarded the fellowship—no one else had competed!

Inasmuch as the Second World War was then in progress, it was not feasible to use the fellowship for study in Germany. It seemed best, therefore, to enroll for the master of theology degree in New Testament at Princeton. Piper had been transferred from theology to New Testament the previous year and had meanwhile developed diversified offerings of New Testament courses. Furthermore, except for a required course titled "Methodology of New Testament Studies," the choice of courses for the master's degree in New Testament was entirely elective. I had found the study of Syriac to be most interesting, and therefore enrolled in Gehman's advanced course involving a study of selections from the Old Syriac Gospels in comparison with the Greek text. Piper offered several courses that were of interest to me: the comparison of the Greek text of the Synoptic Gospels, the Christian interpretation of history, and Greek palaeography (a discipline that he himself had studied under Hans Lietzmann).

---

[4] Oxford: Clarendon, 1915.
[5] Berlin: Reuther & Richard, 1899.

Two other graduate courses were available under a visiting professor from Switzerland. This was Emil Brunner, who offered a most exhilarating series of lectures, "Foundations of Theology," and a course titled "Christ as the Mediator." Of all the lecturers I had ever sat under, I found Brunner to be by far the most dynamic. Though limited to some slight extent as to English vocabulary, his ability to use simple English to express profound thoughts could be electrifying.

The academic year of 1938–39 proved to be an exceptionally busy one, for it was in the autumn of that year that I also began to teach elementary Greek at the Seminary. The opportunity to do so came about in a rather unexpected way. One day in the spring of 1938, some weeks prior to graduation, I happened to sit beside the president of the Seminary, John Mackay, while we were travelling on the train from Princeton to Princeton Junction. Entering into conversation, he invited me to serve as teaching fellow in Greek for the next academic year. Since there had never before been at the Seminary the post of teaching fellow, he needed to explain to me that, while I would be pursuing my own graduate studies, I would also be employed by the Seminary to teach entering students who required instruction in New Testament Greek grammar. Of course I gladly accepted the invitation. In the autumn of 1938, therefore, I began the first of my forty-six years of teaching at Princeton Theological Seminary.

The textbook used in the elementary Greek course was J. Gresham Machen's *New Testament Greek for Beginners*.[6] In addition to the routine of drill in conjugations and declensions, as well as exercises in translation from Greek to English and of English to Greek, it was my custom to introduce from time to time something altogether extraneous to the ordinary assignments in Greek grammar. For example, I might ask if anyone knew which is the shortest verse in the Greek New Testament (it is Luke 20:30 with

---

[6]New York: Macmillan, 1932.

twelve letters), or, what passage contains all the letters of the Greek alphabet (it is 1 Peter 3:19–20).

Because squirrels scamper about on the campus of Princeton Seminary, I might mention that the Greek word for squirrel is *skiouros,* derived from the Greek words *skia* "shadow" and *oura* "tail"—that is, a creature that sits in the shadow of its own tail! On another day I might quote the limerick about a minister who taught Greek to his cat:

> There was a kind curate of Kew
> Who kept a large cat in the pew,
> Which he taught every week
> Alphabetical Greek,
> But got no farther than *mu.*

Besides being the name of the twelfth letter of the Greek alphabet, *mu,* I would explain, is also the vocative form of the Greek word for mouse.

Farther along in the term, I might refer to the etymology of the English word "palindrome," and call attention to the Greek inscription on the rim of the sacred font in the courtyard of Hagia Sophia:

ΝΙΨΟΝΑΝΟΜΗΜΑΜΗΜΟΝΑΝΟΨΙΝ

This can be divided into the words Νίψον ἀνόμημα μὴ μόναν ὄψιν, which can be read forwards and backwards, meaning "Wash your sin not only your face."

Since the second semester of my Th.M. program was drawing to a close, final plans had to be made for the following academic year. The Seminary had announced that a new program of study leading to the Th.D. degree would begin in the autumn. Of course I gave serious consideration to enrolling for this degree. At the same time, however, I also took into account the advantages of the Ph.D. degree in classics at Princeton University. Since I had already taken a variety of biblical courses during my four years at the Seminary, it seemed wise to pursue further work in a related field at another institution. There would still be, I knew, the opportunity to audit additional courses offered by Piper in New Testament.

While still a student at the Seminary, I began to submit articles and book reviews to several journals. My investigation of expressions used by ancient authors to describe plain speaking led to a short article, " 'To Call a Spade a Spade' in Greek and Latin," which was published in the *Classical Journal* in 1938. In the same year the *Christian Century* accepted my review of a significant Festschrift, entitled *Quantulacumque: Studies Presented to Kirsopp Lake.*[7] The following year *Scholastic Magazine* published my discussion of the etymology of English words derived from Arabic in an article I entitled "Words from the Desert." One of the British periodicals that I enjoyed reading in the seminary library was the *Hibbert Journal, A Quarterly Review of Religion, Theology and Philosophy*. The editor, L. P. Jacks, accepted four of my reviews of recently published books in English, French, and German.

Near the close of my Th.M. year I was invited to continue the following year as teaching fellow of New Testament Greek. And so in the autumn of 1939, as I began my fifth year at Princeton, I undertook full-time graduate work at the University while being responsible at the Seminary for teaching three courses: the beginner's two-semester course in Greek, a one-semester review course in Greek for those who had not passed their entrance examination, and a one-hour-per-week review course prescribed for the those who had begun Greek at the Seminary the previous year.

As it happened, the University began that year a new program of study in the Department of Classics. For years the department had offered a combined program in classics and archaeology. Now, quite fortuitously, I was able to enroll in a new program in classics and patristics, under the supervision of Paul R. Coleman-Norton, associate professor of Latin. His interest in the church fathers had earlier led him to study patristics at Christ Church, Oxford, where he

---

[7]Edited by R. P. Casey, S. Lake, and A. K. Lake (London: Christophers, 1937).

presented as his D.Phil. thesis a new edition of the *Dialogus de Vita S. Joannis Chrysostomi* of Palladius.[8]

The syllabus of courses for the new program in patristics overlapped some of the work required of all candidates in classics, but allowed the student to sit for a general examination in church history (up to AD 461) in place of the general examination in Greek history. For the two special authors, one Greek and one Latin, I chose Justin Martyr and Tertullian.

Several other courses besides patristics contributed to preparation in areas that were of intense interest to me. In successive years two visiting professors offered courses that otherwise would not have been available during my time at the University. Ivan Linforth of the University of California, who was then writing his book *The Arts of Orpheus*[9] offered a year's course on Greek religion. Besides having us translate the eschatological myths of Plato, he had us consider the eleventh book of Homer's *Odyssey,* the gold tablets of south Italy and Crete, the paintings of Polygnotus, the sixth book of Virgil's *Aeneid,* and the *Apocalypse of Peter*—all of which present ancient opinions concerning the afterlife of mortals.

The other visiting professor, Henry W. Prescott of the University of Chicago, offered a course in Latin literature in which we read large sections of Apuleius's rollicking narrative known as *Metamorphoses,* or the *Golden Ass,* with its description of cultic reverence shown to the goddess Isis (Book XI).

Three other courses that involved *realia* have also proved to be valuable in more than one respect; these were Duane Reed Stuart's "Latin Inscriptions," Louis B. West's "Greek and Roman Numismatics," and Allen Chester Johnson's "Greek Papyri." Stuart lectured on the history of the investigation of Latin inscriptions and had us read selected items from Dessau's collection. West

---

[8]Cambridge: Cambridge University Press, 1928.
[9]Berkeley: University of California Press, 1941.

introduced us to the specialized handbooks and journals devoted to ancient coins and, by using selected coins from the University's collections, explained how the abbreviated legends and artistic designs on coins served to disseminate political facts and propaganda. Johnson, with only a minimum of preliminary lecturing, had us read selected papyri in various editions. The principal assignment, however, was for each student to decipher, transcribe, and edit with translation and commentary several hitherto unedited papyri in the Princeton University collections. A second-century fragment of Isocrates's *Antidosis* and a magical amulet for curing fevers, dating from the third or fourth century, were allotted to me. Both of these, with my commentary on each, were published later in vol. 3 of *Papyri in the Princeton University Collections.*[10]

Besides other courses in classics, including ancient literary criticism as well as Greek composition and Latin composition, which involved translating pieces of English into those languages according to the style of particular authors, I must not forget to mention what proved to be a most interesting course offered by George W. Elderkin of the Department of Art and Archaeology. This was a seminar on the Graeco-Roman mystery religions. As it happened, no other university student enrolled for the course, but I persuaded two graduate students at the Seminary (Irvin Batdorf and Samuel Moffett) to join me, and Elderkin agreed to conduct the seminar for the three of us.

During the following years, after Elderkin had retired from teaching, I would occasionally offer a seminar on the Graeco-Roman cults for graduate students in the Seminary and in the classics department of the University. Eventually, with the help of fourteen such students I collected and published a classified bibliography embracing 3,647 titles of books and articles on the mystery cults, covering a fifty-year span (see pp. 143–44 below).

---

[10]Princeton: Princeton University Press, 1942.

Before taking the general examinations for the doctoral degree (which at Princeton University are also required for the M.A. degree), it became necessary to give consideration to identifying a subject for the dissertation. Once again it turned out that I was fortunate; I was able to find a project that was acceptable to the Department of Classics and that was also totally in accord with my interests. I proposed to examine palaeographically and textually a Greek lectionary manuscript of the Gospels that had been gathering dust in the library of Princeton Seminary since 1885. It was during April of that year that the Seminary bought the manuscript at a public auction in Paris through the instrumentality of one of her distinguished alumni, Caspar René Gregory. Gregory—who became Charles Hodge's student assistant in 1870, when he also began to compile the index volume to Hodge's three-volume *Systematic Theology*[11]—was one of the few Americans to have become professors in German universities. The Greek manuscript that he acquired for the Seminary contains 340 parchment folios or 680 pages, each more than twelve inches high and ten inches wide. From the style of the handwriting and artistic decoration it appears that the manuscript was written in the twelfth century, probably at or near Constantinople.

An interesting colophon, or note, in Arabic appears in the margin of a page near the beginning of the manuscript and again at its close. According to this duplicated colophon the lectionary had been given to the Church of St. Saba in the diocese of Alexandria. Then follows a curse that would serve as insurance against theft: "No one," warns the colophon, "has authority to remove it from the Church under any condition, and whoever transgresses this will be under the wrath of the eternal word of God, whose power is great. Gregory, Patriarch by the grace of God, wrote this."

Despite the malediction, however, the book was not only removed from the Church of St. Saba, but eventually

---

[11] New York: Scribner's, 1871–73.

made its way to the Monastery of Iveron (whose name shows that it was founded by Iberians, or Georgians) on Mount Athos, where it remained until 1857, when it came into the possession of a Russian archaeologist named Sabastianoff. Twelve years later the great French bibliophile, Ambroise Firmin-Didot, purchased it from Sebastianoff. After Firmin-Didot's death his library was disposed of through a series of auctions. And so the manuscript came to Princeton, where it was awaiting examination by a young Ph.D. candidate in search of hitherto unassessed material suitable for a dissertation. The dissertation, accepted in 1942, was entitled "Studies in a Greek Gospel Lectionary (Gregory 303)."

In order to obtain exposure to a different academic orientation, during the summers of 1940, 1941, and 1942 I visited the University of Chicago and audited lectures in the Divinity School and in the Department of Classics. By this time Edgar J. Goodspeed had retired, but his former students, Donald Riddle, Ernest C. Colwell, and Allen Wikgren, were teaching New Testament in the Divinity School, while Gertrude E. Smith and Jakob A. O. Larsen were offering courses in the field of classics. From all of these I gained new information and stimulating insights, but it was Colwell who helped me most in my research involving Greek lectionaries. During my second summer at Chicago he allowed me to have a key to his study and gave permission to consult the master file of variant readings from previously collated Greek lectionaries. The understanding was that, in return, I would provide for his file the data of variant readings from the Princeton Seminary lectionary—and this I did during my visit to Chicago in the summer of 1942 following my graduation from Princeton University.

In Princeton it was my good fortune to be able to consult occasionally with two other senior professors of New Testament. One of these was James E. Frame, who in 1938 had moved to Princeton after retiring from teaching at Union Theological Seminary in New York. A graduate of the famed Boston Latin School and of Harvard, where he

took a master's degree in Assyrian, he became instructor in
New Testament at Union and eventually Baldwin Professor
of Sacred Literature. Since his Princeton home was located
one block from the seminary campus, in the course of time
I became acquainted with him and would visit him occasionally. Because he was then beginning to be visually
impaired, I suppose that he appreciated talking with visitors. At any rate, I know that I profited greatly from his
reminiscences and observations about lexical and syntacti-
cal problems in the New Testament. For serious study of
the New Testament he had always, by precept and by
example, insisted upon a thorough knowledge of Hebrew
and cognate Semitic languages as an aid to understanding
the deepest thought of the New Testament. I recall his
mentioning to me as his considered opinion that if a student
wished to understand the thought of New Testament writers, and had to choose between studying either Greek or
Hebrew, a case could be made for choosing Hebrew.

Among the books that from time to time Dr. Frame
presented to me was a copy of his *A Critical and Exegetical
Commentary on the Epistles of St. Paul to the Thessalonians* in the
International Critical Commentary series,[12] a book that Dr.
Armstrong had recommended to us as the best commentary
available on the Thessalonian Epistles. Following his recommendation Armstrong mentioned that both Kirsopp Lake
and he had the same opinion about the volume—"and I
guess that makes it so," Armstrong commented with a chuckle.

The other senior New Testament scholar with whom I
became acquainted was William Henry Paine Hatch, professor of the literature and interpretation of the New Testament in the Episcopal Theological School at Cambridge,
Massachusetts. Hatch possessed three earned doctorates:
Ph.D. in classics from Harvard, D.D. from Union Theological Seminary (the only D.D. ever taken in course at Union),
and D.Théol. from Strasbourg. In the early forties, while on
sabbatical leave, Hatch spent several months in Princeton,

---

[12]New York: Scribner's, 1912.

and he and I would frequently meet at lunchtime at the Prince of Orange Restaurant. Thus was laid a foundation for a long-lasting friendship with a great scholar and a man who was totally without guile. Over the years a comment of his that reflects a melancholy realism has stuck in my memory: "It always takes longer than you will think it will take."

Wedding picture of Bruce and Isobel Metzger

The year 1944 is memorable in my life's history; on July 7th of that year Isobel Elizabeth Mackay became my wife. I had made her acquaintance six years before while I was a student at the Seminary and she was pursuing her academic career at Wellesley College, which was followed by graduate study at Columbia University. We were married in Miller Chapel at Princeton Seminary by the bride's father, John A. Mackay, president of the Seminary, assisted by the pastor of the First Presbyterian Church of Princeton, Frank Sargeant Niles. The best man was my friend and colleague Charles T. Fritsch, at that time assistant professor of Old Testament at the Seminary.

Henceforth, and for more than fifty years, I have had the strength and comfort of the most patient and considerate of persons. Indeed, it is impossible to overstate the merits of my wife. Unselfish by nature, she has been able to adapt herself to a variety of different situations. She is hospitable, welcoming, and generous beyond measure.

We have two sons, John Mackay Metzger, born in 1948 and now a lawyer in Trenton specializing in the complexities of tax law, and James Bruce Metzger, born in 1952 and now a physician in Toledo specializing in infectious diseases.

Bruce, James, John, and Isobel Metzger
on holiday in Bermuda, 1992

My marriage has linked me with my wife's Scottish heritage. Over the years it has been possible to make repeated visits to the country of her parents' birth, and thus we have enjoyed the scenery of northern Scotland, and I have been able to become acquainted with her aunts, an uncle, and several cousins.

Chapter 3

EXPANDING HORIZONS

MY acquaintance with a wider spectrum of biblical scholars began in 1937 when, during my second year at seminary, I decided to become a member of the Society of Biblical Literature. This decision came about largely because of a suggestion made by Dr. Gehman, who had taken an interest in me as a fellow Pennsylvanian. In those days the annual meetings of the Society were held during the Christmas vacation period at Union Theological Seminary in New York, and thus it was convenient for Princeton residents to attend the sessions. It goes without saying that I found it both stimulating and enlightening to hear scholars such as William H. P. Hatch, Kirsopp Lake, and Ernest Colwell discuss textual problems.

On one occasion an altercation that generated more heat than light followed the reading of a paper by Donald Riddle of the University of Chicago in which he criticized sharply the view held by C. C. Torrey of Yale, namely that the Greek Gospels are translations of Aramaic originals. During the discussion period, Torrey, a patrician figure, refused to be drawn into the debate and haughtily declared that he did not see anyone present who knew enough Aramaic to make such a debate profitable!

After having attended several such annual sessions I began to venture to offer papers myself, starting in 1941 with a summary of the research for my dissertation, "Notes on the Saturday and Sunday Lessons from Luke in Greek Gospel Lectionaries." In the following years the subjects of my papers went further afield: "The Relationship of the Palestinian Syriac Lectionary to the Greek Lectionary System" (1942); "A Survey of the Investigation of the Caesarean Text of the Gospels" (1943); "St. Jerome's Testimony concerning the Second Grade of Mithraic Initiation" (1944); "Trends in the Textual Criticism of the Iliad, the Mahābhārata, and the New Testament" (1945); and "Tatian's Diatessaron and a Persian Harmony of the Gospels" (1949). The paper on Mithraism was so far removed from the biblical field that, instead of submitting it to the *Journal of Biblical Literature,* I sent it to the *American Journal of Philology,* where, in due time, it was published. The point of the paper was to show that Mithraism, instead of being a more or less unified cult, as many writers had assumed, actually differed in doctrine and practice in various parts of the Roman Empire.

In 1944 the research embodied in my dissertation, put into the context of data from the Chicago master-file of lectionary readings, was published by the University of Chicago Press under the title *The Saturday and Sunday Lessons from Luke in the Greek Gospel Lectionary,* being no. 3 of vol. 2 in the series, Studies in the Lectionary Text of the Greek New Testament.

During the following months I began collecting information for another publication, entitled *Lexical Aids for Students of New Testament Greek.* The first part of this book lists words of the vocabulary of the Greek New Testament according to the frequency of their occurrence, ranging from those that occur more than five hundred times and decreasing to words that occur ten times. Following the English definitions are also such English derivatives from the Greek as may be of assistance in remembering the meaning of the Greek words. The second part of the book exhibits the family relationships among words of frequent occurrence. The work of compilation involved the laborious task of counting the number of citations of each word in Moulton and Geden's concordance to the Greek New Testament—information that today can be obtained quickly by means of a computer.

My next task was to prepare on a Vari-Typer each page for photographic reproduction and printing by lithography. But, alas! the several publishers to whom I submitted the material were not persuaded that the book would sell, and one by one returned the sample pages to me. Finally, and somewhat in desperation, I decided to undertake issuing the book myself, and in 1946 I had fifteen hundred copies printed at Ypsilanti, Michigan. Some years later, after the book had become known through reviews, a second printing was called for. Eventually many more reprintings were made, and copies were distributed through the Theological Book Agency at Princeton, as well as in British printings issued first by Blackwells of Oxford and later by T. & T. Clark of Edinburgh (1990). It is really amazing to me that, as of this writing, more than two hundred thousand copies, not including unknown numbers in Korean, Malagasy, and Portuguese (Brazilian) translations, have been distributed.

Several years after the publication of *Lexical Aids* and in view of a growing interest in America in the Coptic language, it occurred to me that a similar frequency wordlist might prove useful for students who were beginning the study of that language. Consequently, during my spare time I began to compile, on the basis of Michel Wilmet's monumental *Concordance du Nouveau Testament sahidique*, graduated lists of Coptic words. As compared with a total of 1,055 Greek words (other than proper names) that occur ten times or more in the Greek New Testament, there are only 643 Coptic words used ten times or more in the Sahidic New Testament. In 1961 a pamphlet entitled *Lists of Words Occurring Frequently in the Coptic New Testament (Sahidic Dialect)* was set up in type and issued by E. J. Brill of Leiden; it was reprinted in 1962 by William B. Eerdmans, Grand Rapids.

Another kind of literary work was laid on my shoulders from 1945 until 1959, during which time I served as editorial secretary of the theological quarterly, *Theology Today,* a journal begun in 1944 by the president of Princeton Seminary, John A. Mackay. My chief task was that of proofreader, but as time went on, more than once I also did copyediting of manuscripts submitted for publication.

One such article, however, proved virtually impossible to correct without violating the author's intent. This was a hitherto unpublished sermon that Phillips Brooks had preached in Trinity Church, Boston, on December 19, 1886. The manuscript, entitled "A Sermon on the Nature of the Church," had been given by Mrs. Herbert A. Hawkins of Worcester, Massachusetts, a niece of Bishop Brooks, to Dr. Earl L. Douglass, a resident of Princeton. The text of the sermon was Matthew 28:20, "And, lo, I am with you alway, even unto the end of the world." Overlooking that Matthew places these words as spoken by Jesus in Galilee (28:16), and that according to Acts the Ascension took place at the Mount of Olives near Jerusalem, Brooks began his sermon: "These are the last words which Jesus spoke on earth. A few moments after He had spoken them, He passed out of His Disciples' sight and mortal eyes have never seen Him again as He was then beheld." It was finally decided to allow Brooks's anachronistic statement to remain in the printed form of the sermon.[1]

Occasional invitations to give lectures outside Princeton broadened my horizons. Early in 1945 I received a letter from Dr. Wolf Leslau, a specialist in Ethiopic, inviting me to participate in a series of nine weekly lectures at the Ecole libre des hautes études (a temporary home for exiled European scholars sponsored by the New School for Social Research in New York City). The proposed series, entitled "The Semitic Literatures of the Near East," was intended, he wrote, "chiefly for a wide public, although the subject of each of them is to be dealt with by a scholar of high reputation. We should be extremely happy if you would deliver one of these lectures, on the subject 'The Syriac Literature.' Lectures can be delivered in French or in English." Highly pleased—not to say flattered—by Leslau's letter, I did not delay in accepting the invitation.

---

[1] *Theology Today* 12 (1955) 57.

Another invitation that pleased me even more came at the close of the 1940s when I was asked to present a popular lecture at Yale University on "St. Jerome and the Vulgate." The lecture, one of a series proposed (I think) by Dr. Heinz Bluhm, who had published research on Luther's German translation of the Bible, was intended for the general public, and I was cautioned against making it overly technical.

About thirty or forty persons were present that evening as I attempted to show the pervasive influence exerted by Jerome's Latin Vulgate not only in the sphere of religion but also in secular culture through the development of Latin into the Romance languages. During the question period at the close of the lecture a listener reproached me for making what she had taken to be a disparagement of Roman Catholicism. I was altogether surprised by the interpretation put on the point I had made, and attempted to restate what I had intended to convey. The incident taught me to be more heedful in the future when addressing a diversified audience.

In the opening months of 1948 an invitation came to me to participate in a conference later that year which, as it turned out, was eventually to open many doors. Planned by Dr. Colwell and other colleagues at the University of Chicago, the conference was scheduled to be held October 22 and 23 at the Divinity School of the university. The purpose of the gathering was twofold: to honor Emeritus Professor Edgar J. Goodspeed and to discuss matters preliminary to the preparation of a comprehensive critical apparatus of the Greek New Testament. The overall subject announced for consideration was "New Testament Manuscript Study," with a focus on "The Materials and the Making of a Critical Apparatus."

As president of the university, Colwell presided at the opening session of the conference. The first speaker was the learned and charming Mlle Sirarpie Der Nersessian of Dumbarton Oaks in Washington; she presented a paper titled "Illustration of Armenian MSS of the New Testament as Exemplified in the American Collections." This was

Ernest Cadman Colwell

followed by an examination of "The Narrative and Liturgical Gospel Illustration" in Greek manuscripts, presented by Kurt Weitzmann of Princeton University. These two papers dealt with the making of deluxe New Testament manuscripts. The concluding paper of the opening session was an evaluation of "The Importance of the Michigan Manuscript Collection for Textual Studies." This was presented by Dr. Merrill M. Parvis, who for some years had been Colwell's assistant.

The second session began with the dedication of the University of Chicago's collection of New Testament manuscripts. Following the ceremony of dedication, which was conducted by Harold H. Swift, chairman of the board of trustees of the university, two papers were presented by those who, over the years, had been largely instrumental in developing the collection. Edgar J. Goodspeed, in his inimitable style, spoke about "Adventures with Manuscripts." He had begun his graduate work at Yale in Semitics but later enrolled at the newly established University of Chicago where he subsequently heard a series of lectures by a visiting scholar from Germany, Caspar René Gregory, on the Greek manuscripts of the New Testament—and the course of his life was completely reoriented.

From that time onward Goodspeed devoted himself to collecting, studying, and editing manuscripts of the Greek New Testament. Among the many manuscripts that he had been instrumental in acquiring for the University of Chicago's growing collection was one with the unusual sobriquet, "the Gangsters' Bible," given it by newspaper reporters. This was a late copy of the four Gospels in Greek, once in the possession of a Chicago band of gangsters. When new members were sworn into membership of the gang, they would touch this copy of the Scriptures and swear an oath that they would never betray other members of the group.

Much more important was the acquisition of an unusual Byzantine manuscript of the Gospels sumptuously illustrated with almost one hundred exquisitely executed paintings. This, the Rockefeller McCormick New Testament, had been edited in three volumes by Goodspeed along with Harold R. Willoughby and Donald Riddle. One of the interesting details of the codex is a colophon scrawled on its last flyleaf, conveying the curse of the 318 Holy Fathers assembled at Nicea upon anyone who should ever steal the book from the church or convent to which it was being given. Among the several books and articles that the Rockefeller McCormick codex stimulated was a mystery novel written by Goodspeed and entitled *The Curse of the Colophon*.[2] Following Goodspeed's presentation, the second paper, by Colwell, recounted "The Story of the Collection."

---

[2] Chicago: Willett, Clark & Co., 1935.

The lectures on the following day of the conference were focussed on the sources available for editing the text of the Greek New Testament. The first speaker was Kenneth W. Clark of Duke University; his subject was "The MSS of the Greek New Testament." It was altogether appropriate that he should deal with that subject, for in the early thirties Clark had earned his Ph.D. degree at the University of Chicago with a dissertation that comprised a descriptive catalogue listing and describing all of the known New Testament Greek manuscripts in America at that time—a total of 256.

Not only did Clark possess firsthand information as to what was available in museums, libraries, and private collections in the United States but he was knowledgeable also concerning auctions held in Europe and elsewhere where Greek manuscripts were offered for sale. Given his command of such information, it is not surprising that the rare-book room of Duke University began to acquire a collection of Greek manuscripts second only to that at Chicago. Clark's future work along these lines was to take him to St. Catherine's monastery on Mount Sinai and to the libraries of the Greek and the Armenian patriarchates in Jerusalem; at these places he supervised the microfilming of several thousand manuscripts for the Library of Congress, totalling about twenty miles of film.

I was next on the program; the subject that had been assigned to me was "The Versional Evidence for the Text of the New Testament." Within the limits of the time allotted, I dealt with the significance of ancient versions for textual studies of the New Testament. The chief versions are those in Latin, Syriac, and Coptic; the secondary versions include the Gothic, Armenian, Georgian, Ethiopic, and Old Church Slavonic.

The speaker who followed me was Robert P. Casey of Brown University; his subject was "The Patristic Evidence for the Text of the New Testament." Casey's earlier training had prepared him well to deal with this topic. After his education at Boston Latin School he received the A.B. and

S.T.B. degrees from Harvard. Next he spent two years at Jesus College, Cambridge, where his dissertation, "Studies in Clement of Alexandria," was accepted for the Ph.D. degree in 1924. Later, Casey was associated with Kirsopp Lake on the advisory board of Lake's series, Studies and Documents, in which Casey published several monographs himself.

At the fourth and final session of the conference, three papers were presented that dealt with assessing the task of collecting evidence from Greek manuscripts, early versions, and patristic citations in the making of a comprehensive *apparatus criticus*. The speakers who successively addressed these three areas were Frederick C. Grant of Union Theological Seminary, Allen P. Wikgren of the University of Chicago, and Robert M. Grant of the University of the South.[3] All agreed that the work was greatly needed and would require many collaborators in order to be accomplished. But the story of how such a project was undertaken must be told in another chapter (see pages 56–66 below).

---

[3]The several papers presented during the conference were subsequently published in Merrill M. Parvis and Allen P. Wikgren, eds., *New Testament Manuscript Studies* (Chicago: University of Chicago Press, 1950).

Chapter 4

ORDINATION AND VOCATION
IN CHURCH AND SEMINARY

URING my senior year at Princeton Theological Seminary, and after satisfying the requirements prescribed
by the Presbyterian Church in the U.S.A., in April of
1938 I was licensed by the Presbytery of New Brunswick
(New Jersey) "to preach the Gospel of Christ, as a proba-
tioner for the holy ministry." This was the first stage in the
process of seeking ordination. The following year, on April
11, 1939, the same Presbytery ordained me as an evangelist.
The category of ordination as an evangelist was, at that
time, prescribed for someone who was expecting to serve,
not as the pastor of a local congregation, but as a teacher or
chaplain in an institution. Both categories of ordination
entailed the same prerogatives and authority to administer
the sacraments and to perform marriages.

Although I have not served as the settled pastor of a
local church, I have, in fact, officiated at several weddings,
as well as conducted funerals and memorial services. Chiefly,
however, it has been my privilege over the years to preach
at Sunday services of worship and to present Bible studies
in churches belonging to a wide variety of denominations.
The total number of such services and lectures has now
exceeded twenty-five hundred.

Among the several Bible studies that congregations
seemed to appreciate most were expositions of the Sermon
on the Mount and, especially, the book of Revelation.
Depending upon the wishes of the local congregation, such

lectures were presented on successive days or evenings of a week or on Sundays of successive weeks. Quite unusual was the request of the Council of Churches at Albuquerque, New Mexico, that I present in September of 1990 a series of seven one-hour lectures on Revelation during one day (a Saturday). At the close of the series most of the hearers must have been weary—I know that I was both weary and hoarse.

The longest series of repeated invitations to preach from the same pulpit began in 1960 when Dr. Frank Gaebelein, the founder and headmaster of the Stony Brook School for Boys, located at Stony Brook, Long Island, invited me to participate in the Sunday morning service of worship in the school's Hageman Chapel. For thirty-five years thereafter I returned annually to deliver a sermon suitable for the season during the academic term.

My contacts with Dr. Gaebelein led to my being invited by the Council for Religion in Independent Schools to write a textbook containing basic information about the New Testament and its historical background. In 1965 the book was published with the title *The New Testament: Its Background, Growth, and Content.*[1] Issued in an enlarged second edition in 1983, over the years it has been widely adopted as a textbook for upper forms in schools as well as for first and second year courses in colleges.

My chief service to the church has been, of course, teaching prospective ministers enrolled in a theological seminary. During a period of forty-six years I served successively at Princeton Seminary as teaching fellow (1938–40), instructor in New Testament (1940–44), assistant professor (1944–48), associate professor (1948–54), professor (1954–64), and finally as George L. Collord Professor of New Testament Language and Literature (1964–84).[2] In 1984, when I

---

[1] Nashville: Abingdon.

[2] Mr. Collord was a Presbyterian industrialist residing at Pittsburgh, Pennsylvania; he also endowed a chair of religion at Princeton University.

had reached the age of seventy, retirement was mandatory, and I became Professor Emeritus.

During the nearly half a century of teaching seminary students my academic interests broadened. Moving from courses dealing with linguistics and historical sources bearing on the religious and social background of the New Testament period, I developed exegetical courses on a variety of New Testament books. For many years I taught the required introductory New Testament course. During the absence of Dr. Piper one year I was asked to teach his elective course on New Testament theology. Over a good many years, in alternating semesters I taught courses on the Sermon on the Mount, the person and the work of Christ, the parables of Jesus, the Epistle to the Hebrews, and the life and literature of the early church. By offering occasionally a practicum on spirituality and the devotional life, as well as by critiquing during one semester the sermons preached by seniors, I was brought into contact with what are commonly regarded as the more "practical" aspects of theological training.

As for my graduate courses and seminars, these dealt with Greek palaeography, textual criticism, the Graeco-Roman mystery religions, the canon of the New Testament, Syriac patristics, and Coptic.

All told, over the years I developed twenty-five different courses and seminars. The one that I enjoyed most was "Survey and Methodology of New Testament Study," required of Th.M. candidates specializing in New Testament. During this course students were introduced firsthand to a variety of ancient sources, both Jewish and pagan, including papyri, coins, inscriptions, and the Mishnah, and were required to write a detailed critical review of a modern monograph of their own choosing. An adequate book review, I urged, should do three things: describe the book, communicate something of its quality, and pass judgment on it. A copy of the review, made available to each student in the class, enabled the others to become acquainted with a wide variety of important studies. For the preparation of the paper the student was to acquire and follow William Strunk's admirable paperback *Elements of Style*—a book that Dean Weigle had recommended for my study when I became a member of the Standard Bible Committee. In 1950, in order to aid graduate students, I drew up a pamphlet entitled *A Guide to the Preparation of a Thesis,* which was published by the Seminary.

Besides lecturing and attending to the usual chores of correcting examination papers and attending faculty meetings (where it is customary to keep minutes and to waste hours!), a variety of other opportunities to serve the church presented themselves. One such opportunity came in the latter part of the 1940s when I served on a committee undertaking the revision of a document called the Intermediate Catechism. This catechism, which had been adopted in 1912 by the General Assembly of the Presbyterian Church in the U.S.A., was intended to be simpler in language than the Shorter Catechism prepared by the Westminster Divines in the seventeenth century.

One of the promoters of such a revision was Dr. Earl L. Douglass, who for years had been publishing in scores of newspapers a syndicated column of an inspirational nature, as well as writing an annual volume of exposition of the biblical passages used in the International Sunday School Lessons. Following his retirement from earlier pastorates, and having moved to Princeton, Douglass served as chairman of the catechism revision committee, which was made up of several pastors and the following seminary personnel: Elmer G. Homrighausen, professor of Christian education; Hugh T. Kerr, Jr., associate professor of theology; Lefferts A. Loetscher, assistant professor of church history; and two members of the biblical department, Charles T. Fritsch, assistant professor of Old Testament, and myself.

The task assigned to us was to prepare a simple yet comprehensive account of the Christian faith in question and answer format. Eventually we produced a list of sixty-nine questions and answers arranged in eight sections. These were headed (1) Our Knowledge of God; (2) Man and His

Sin; (3) Christ Our Savior; (4) Repentance and Faith; (5) The Church and the Kingdom; (6) The Means of Grace; (7) The Christian Life; and (8) The Future Life.

The kind of questions and answers included in the catechism can be seen from the following:

Q. 1. What is the most important thing in life?
A. The most important thing in life is to know God and to obey His will.

Q. 2. How do we know God?
A. We know God in part by the revelation of Himself in the world which He has created, but He gives us a saving knowledge of Himself only in the Bible which the Holy Spirit enables us to understand.

Q. 48. What is prayer?
A. Prayer is communion with God in the name of Jesus Christ, in which, alone or with others, we tell God of our love for Him, our sorrow for our sins, our thankfulness for His gifts, our desires for ourselves and others, and our dedication to His will.

Q. 49. What help does God promise us when we pray?
A. When we pray God assures us of His guiding presence and forgiving love, of His provision for our daily needs, and of His willingness to answer our prayers as is best for us and His kingdom.

In due time our work was published as a ten-page booklet entitled *An Outline of the Christian Faith in Question and Answer Form.* [3] For some years it was distributed by the Board of Christian Education of the Presbyterian Church, but subsequently, owing to the lack of emphasis on catechetical training, it went out of print.

An opportunity to be involved more closely in ecclesiastical matters came to me in 1957 when I was elected,

---

[3]Philadelphia: Published for the General Assembly by the Board of Christian Education of the Presbyterian Church in the United States of America, 1948.

along with two other members of the seminary faculty, to represent the Presbytery of New Brunswick at the 169th General Assembly of the Presbyterian Church, held that year at Omaha, Nebraska. Each of the 171 presbyteries is entitled to elect an equal number of ministers and laity in proportion to the number of communicant members in that presbytery.

It was an educational experience for me to participate with several hundred other commissioners, as they are called, during eight days of deliberations of the highest court of the denomination. The number and variety of reports brought to the floor of the assembly for consideration seemed to be without end.

During the 1950s discussion was taking place in various parts of the Presbyterian Church over the question whether the study of Hebrew and Greek should continue to be required as prerequisite to ordination to the Gospel ministry. In 1958 the Curriculum Committee, Council on Theological Education, appointed a subcommittee to study the relationship of courses involving the biblical languages to the Bachelor of Divinity curriculum as a whole. Several of us on the subcommittee, representing Louisville, McCormick, and Princeton seminaries, sent out questionnaires to graduates of the previous five years, inquiring how far and in what respects they considered their study of Hebrew and Greek to have been, or not to have been, beneficial for the work in the active ministry. A substantial majority of those who responded indicated that they thought they had profited from gaining an acquaintance of the biblical languages, and said they favored retaining the current language requirement for ordination.

In 1962 the subcommittee issued its report on "The Biblical Languages in Theological Education: Theological and Practical Implications." Among the seven chapters of the report, David Noel Freedman dealt with "The Hebrew Old Testament and the Minister Today," and I dealt with "The Greek New Testament and the Minister Today." Other chapters included "The Reformed View of the Word of God" by Cornelius De Boe and "Faith and Language in the Church" by Joseph Haroutunian.

Several years later the General Assembly of the Presbyterian Church directed all presbyteries to consider whether or not the study of Hebrew and Greek should be made optional for ordination. It goes without saying that I was pleased when a majority voted that the Church should continue to require them.

Another committee of the Presbyterian Church on which I was invited to serve was a special committee on the work of the Holy Spirit. Appointed by the 180th General Assembly in 1968, this committee was requested to study the work of the Holy Spirit with special reference to speaking in tongues (glossolalia) and other charismatic gifts within the fellowship of the United Presbyterian Church (U.S.A.). During the previous years a number of clergy and laity had become involved in charismatic experiences that had sometimes led to dissension within a local congregation. When pastors became involved, the pastoral relationship had occasionally been terminated. When lay people became involved in charismatic experiences, they often felt alienated from their pastor and from other non-charismatic church members. It was to analyze and address such problems that a committee was convened by the moderator of the General Assembly, Dr. John Coventry Smith.

The eleven members of the committee included three pastors (Rev. John Strock, who served as chair; Rev. David H. C. Read, who was responsible for drawing together the recommendations of the committee; and Rev. Jack M. Chisholm), a physician (Dr. Thomas Foster), a psychologist (Dr. Charles H. Meisgeier), a Navy chaplain (T. David Parham), two lay persons (James D. Copeland and Phil W. Jordan), and two biblical scholars (David E. Dilworth of Whitworth College and myself). Two of the members of the committee were themselves charismatic and had spoken in tongues.

After several meetings, which were held in a motel near the airport at St. Louis, it became apparent that another year would be needed before the committee would be able to submit a final report. A variety of persons had been invited to provide information to the committee. We heard from Thomas F. Zimmerman, the general superintendent of the Assemblies of God denomination, and David du Plessis, the acknowledged "father" of modern Pentecostalism. Several Presbyterians also appeared before our committee, including the president of San Francisco Theological Seminary, Dr. Arnold C. Come, who had published a book entitled *Human Spirit and Holy Spirit.*[4] His recommendation to the committee was brief and to the point: "Speaking in tongues is not Presbyterian; therefore, those who speak in tongues should be invited to leave the church"—or, as someone put it, should be given the left foot of fellowship!

In the following year, after three more meetings had been held, the committee made its report to the 182nd General Assembly (1970). The report was drawn up in several sections; the first was exegetical and examined the scriptural references to the Holy Spirit in general and the passages on the "gifts of the Spirit" in some detail. This was followed by three other sections, entitled "Some Theological Considerations," "Psychological Dimensions," and, by way of conclusion, "Guidelines." This final section provided suggestions addressed to ministers and to laity, both those who had had Neo-Pentecostal experiences and those who had not had such experiences.

The tenor of the entire report is summed up in the final paragraph of the exegetical section:

> We therefore conclude, on the basis of Scripture, that the practice of glossolalia should be neither despised nor forbidden; on the other hand it should not be emphasized nor made normative for the Christian experience. Generally the experience should be private, and those who have experienced a genuine renewal of their faith in this way should be on guard against divisiveness within the congregation. At

---

[4]Philadelphia: Westminster, 1959.

the same time those who have received no unusual experiences of the Holy Spirit should be alert to the possibility of deeper understanding of the gospel and a fuller participation in the gifts of the Spirit—of which love is the greatest.

The report was accepted in 1970 by the 182nd General Assembly of the United Presbyterian Church (U.S.A.) and made available in pamphlet format. In this form the first twenty-eight pages present the report itself and pages 29 to 56 incorporate two appendixes of more lengthy discussions concerning "The Holy Spirit in the New Testament" (dealing with three themes, "The So-Called Baptism with the Holy Spirit," "Gifts of the Spirit," and "Speaking in Tongues") and "A More Detailed Summary of Relevant Psychological Literature." In the years following the availability of the report, the denomination experienced fewer disruptions of order and decorum in services of worship, but how much this was due to the influence of the report I am unable to say.

Toward the close of my teaching career a new form of communication became available—video recording. In 1991 I was invited to lead the Bible study hour for three days at the meeting of the General Board of Discipleship of the United Methodist Church held at Nashville. My presentations, which were on selected parts of the book of Revelation, must have suggested to editors of the Abingdon Press that a longer and fuller series of such studies might be useful for adult Bible class discussions. After negotiations as to the number and length of such presentations, a series of eight video segments was prepared with the title *Breaking the Code: Understanding the Book of Revelation.* Accompanying the video was a leader's guide, prepared by Donn Downall, and a 110–page paperback book with the same title, in which I set out a more detailed exposition. The book was also made available separately.

The office of Video-Media Services at Princeton Theological Seminary has included among its offerings several of my presentations and discussions, aimed at assisting pastors and congregations. They include "Practical Ways to Increase Biblical Literacy," "Questions from Colleagues in

Ministry," and a two-part interview with Dr. Kathy Nelson on "Biblical Origins of Christmas."

During the years following my retirement it happened that a totally different area of service opened up when I received letters from prisoners in penal institutions. Three such cases come to mind.

An inmate at a correctional institution in Jefferson City, Missouri, wrote more than once with questions about the books of the Apocrypha, and why they are differently regarded by different churches. These queries led to further questions about the Qumran manuscripts found in caves by the Dead Sea. In both cases I tried to provide the inquirer with information that I hoped would clarify matters that had been perplexing him.

Another prisoner sent a letter addressed to me, in care of The Oxford University Press, New York City, that began as follows: "Dear Bruce, I am writing to you from the Oklahoma State Penitentiary, where I am doing 26 life-sentences for a string of 30 armed robberies I committed in December of 1990 (fortunately nobody was ever hurt or killed)." Three pages closely written on both sides told an amazing story, the gist of which was that, "having been raised in an agnostic—if not atheist—environment," he "found God" through repeated discussions with his cell-mate, a Christian believer. Subsequently he began to study a copy of Machen's *New Testament Greek for Beginners*, a book which, at the time of writing to me, he had nearly completed. He indicated his desire to obtain a copy of the Greek New Testament, with a lexicon, as well as other biblical helps.

Consequently I had the Princeton Seminary book agency mail him several different volumes, including my own copy of *The Jerome Biblical Commentary* (the penitentiary will not accept parcels sent to inmates by private individuals). In subsequent letters to me Tom (that is not his real name) occasionally included quotations of verses from the Greek text of the New Testament, written in a clear and regular minuscule—better than mine is usually!

After several months of corresponding with Tom my last letters went unanswered. I learned from his cell-mate, Fred (that is not his real name), that Tom had been moved to another part of the penitentiary, and that they were no longer in touch with each other. I have thought that perhaps he may have been moved to the infirmary, for in one of his letters he had mentioned his almost constant pain, and made the comment: "I will never be an octogenarian, like yourself. I'm only 28 but I have Crohn's disease; it's an inflammatory bowel disorder, chronic, and has already caused me to lose 10 ft. of my intestines." It may be that the disease, described by *The Merck Manual* as "baffling," was in his case fatal.

My correspondence with Tom's cell-mate has continued from the summer of 1994 when, at Tom's suggestion, I sent a birthday card to Fred, who, he said, had been feeling somewhat disconsolate. From Fred's subsequent letters I learned that, having been born in 1965 in what would perhaps be described as a dysfunctional family, at the age of twelve Fred became a ward of the state of Maine because he had been physically abused. The following year he burglarized a house and was put on probation. For the next two years he was in several foster homes, but because he had stolen a firearm and had violated his probation, he was sentenced to a detention center until his eighteenth birthday.

After his release Fred roamed as a vagabond, sleeping in county jails and surviving by panhandling. Following several run-ins with the law, he was sentenced to the Oklahoma Department of Corrections for six years. Because of bad behavior, the next year he was sent to the Oklahoma State Penitentiary. Later that year Fred became involved in a riot in which he assisted others in taking over a control room within the prison. In the melee he had assaulted a correctional officer. The riot then spread to different parts of the prison, and the governor of the state declared an emergency. The national guard and several law enforcement agencies surrounded the prison, regaining possession of the prison and "locking it down"—to use Fred's own phrase.

An old cell house of the prison that had been con-
demned by a federal judge was reopened, and Fred, along
with others, was placed there under tight security. I will let
Fred continue in his own words:

> While there in the East Cell House just before Christmas [in
> 1985], I received a letter at mail call. (Now up to this time I
> had never gotten a letter, if I remember correctly.) The
> return address read, "From a concerned citizen." I opened
> the letter and inside was a Christian tract entitled, "God's
> Simple Plan of Salvation." My heart was gripped with fear
> and trembling, and for the first time in my life I sensed
> the "reality" of hell and realized that if I were to die I was
> going to hell! This was the turning point as I can now see in
> retrospect. . . .
>
> In February of 1986 I gave my life to Christ. Two months
> later I received my G.E.D.—G.E.D. means general educa-
> tion development—it is an equivalent to a high school
> diploma and is accepted as such throughout the United
> States. I had never stepped foot inside high school, and so I
> was surprised when I passed the test.
>
> From 1986–88 I completed several Bible studies, receiving 15
> or 16 Bible Certificates. Then from 1989–91 I was in a kind of
> slump. I can't explain why but during that time my spiritual
> life was in a low estate. I was tired of the shallow, non-
> intellectual presentation of Christianity with which I was
> surrounded. I knew that I needed something to get me over
> this slump. I desired to hear and to be around the intellec-
> tual presentation of the Gospel. In May of 1991 I was
> enrolled into The Omega School of Theology [a correspon-
> dence school in Maryland]. It was also about that time that I
> began to study N.T. Greek grammar. I began with Machen's
> *New Testament Greek for Beginners.* My spiritual life improved
> 100%! By the time I had finished Machen's grammar I knew
> that I wanted to become a N.T. Scholar.

A Christian friend had been sending Fred a money
order every month so that he could buy snacks at the
commissary—pretzels, potato chips, candy bars, and the
like. In December of 1991, and with the approval of his
friend, Fred began to use the money to purchase a number

of standard works from Christian Book Distributors, Peabody, Massachusetts. These included the Greek text of the
Apostolic Fathers and of Eusebius's *Ecclesiastical History* as
well as such grammatical and lexical works as A. T. Robertson's huge Greek grammar, Moulton and Geden's Greek
concordance, the third edition of the Bible Societies' *Greek
New Testament,* with the textual commentary, the Bauer-
Arndt-Gingrich Greek-English lexicon, the four volumes of
Moulton-Howard-Turner's Greek grammar,[5] and several of
my own books published by the Oxford University Press (it
was information from the title page of one of the latter that
prompted Tom, his cell-mate, to address his first letter to
me as he did).

In November of 1994 Fred inquired of me what studies
he would need to undertake in order to prepare himself to
teach New Testament Greek. I indicated that certainly a
reading knowledge of German and Latin would be prerequisite for advanced study, and to get him started I sent some
elementary helps for learning German. He thanked me and
said that he would make good use of them. Three months
later I was pleased to receive a letter from him composed in
generally accurate and idiomatic German. I then sent him a
Latin grammar, a Latin dictionary, and a copy of the
Vulgate Bible—as well as a copy of *The Oxford Classical
Dictionary.*[6]

---

[5] *The Apostolic Fathers* (Loeb Classical Library; Cambridge:
Harvard University Press, 1965); Eusebius, *The Ecclesiastical History*
(Loeb Classical Library; Cambridge: Harvard University Press,
1932); A. T. Robertson, *A Grammar of the Greek New Testament in the
Light of Historical Research* (5th ed.; New York: Richard R. Smith,
1931); W. F. Moulton and A. S. Geden, *A Concordance to the Greek
Testament* (Edinburgh: T. & T. Clark, 1914); *A Greek-English Lexicon
of the New Testament and Other Early Christian Literature* (2d ed.;
Chicago: University of Chicago Press, 1979); James Hope Moul-
ton, *A Grammar of New Testament Greek* (4 vols.; Edinburgh: T. &
T. Clark, 1908–76).

[6] Edited by N. G. L. Hammond et al.; 2d ed.; Oxford:
Clarendon, 1972.

In a recent letter, after mentioning that he had now acquired nearly sixty books, Fred commented as follows:

> In 1992 when I went on a book-buying spree I was buying at random. I just barely had a knowledge of Greek, which was definitely imperfect at that time. I bought them with the belief that I could work my way into them. Strengthened by the grace of God I began to climb this "mountain of difficulty," seeking to understand. It was not until later, when I had a better knowledge of Greek, that it dawned on me that I had collected together books by authors who were essentially of one mind. . . . I had, so-to-speak, collected together a "family" of like-minded scholars. Was that by chance or by design? In retrospect, I personally believe that I was led by the Holy Spirit in choosing the books I chose.

In the autumn of 1996 Fred completed the final comprehensive examination of the correspondence course with the Omega School of Theology. Some weeks later he sent me the letter he had received from the president of the school. This conveyed "hearty congratulations on having completed the Bachelor of Theology Program with an outstanding grade point average of 99.71 *(summa cum laude)*."

By the year 2000, when Fred is due for discharge, he will be in his mid-thirties. After he has become acclimated to freedom once again, one trusts that he will go forward in fulfilling his dream of becoming a teacher of New Testament Greek. I am happy to have had some small part in directing his preliminary preparation for attaining that goal.

Chapter 5

THE INTERNATIONAL GREEK NEW TESTAMENT PROJECT

URING the twentieth century, scholars kept bringing to light previously unknown New Testament manuscripts. Thus the record of variant readings Tischendorf cited in his famous eighth edition of 1869–72 became more and more in need of updating. The International Greek New Testament Project is a descriptive title given to a project that undertook just such an updating.

This was not the first attempt to assemble these newly found variant readings. In the mid-1920s several British and German scholars considered the feasibility of compiling a major new critical apparatus, as full and accurate as possible. Differences of opinion, however, as to the choice of the base against which the manuscripts should be collated prevented international cooperation.

Meanwhile a committee of several British scholars was pressing forward under the Reverend S. C. E. Legg as editor and issued through the Clarendon Press at Oxford two volumes, one containing an apparatus to the Gospel according to Mark (1935) and the other, a similar apparatus for Matthew (1940). Both volumes, however, evoked severe and widespread criticism as to the accuracy as well as adequacy of citation of patristic evidence. Consequently, the committee, upon receiving in 1948 Legg's manuscript on Luke, decided they could not recommend its publication.

It is not surprising that when, at a 1948 conference of New Testament scholars in Chicago, Dr. Colwell broached the proposal that an international team of scholars be formed in order to produce a comprehensive apparatus for the Greek New Testament, the proposal was met with hearty endorsement. Prior to the conference George D. Kilpatrick of Oxford, one of the chief British textual scholars, had written to Dr. Colwell, inquiring as to whether American scholars would be willing to assist in the preparation of a critical apparatus that British scholars had already begun to collect. This was the beginning of what came to be the International Greek New Testament Project.

In December of 1948, at the business session of the annual meeting of the Society of Biblical Literature, Colwell outlined the scope of the proposed project and sought the endorsement of the society as well as authorization for the creation of a temporary planning commission to set up such editorial boards and committees as it would see fit. This proposal was approved by the society.

During the spring of 1949, and supported by a grant from the Rockefeller Foundation for the work of organization, Kilpatrick was brought to Chicago in order to confer with several American textual scholars. It was decided that an American and a British committee should collaborate in undertaking the production of what could be called a thesaurus of variant readings of the text of the New Testament.

Later that year Dr. Merrill Parvis was sent to England as a representative of American scholars. As a result of this interchange and discussion substantial agreement was reached on several major questions of policy and procedure. It was decided that, in view of the availability of the Legg's volumes on Matthew and Mark—despite their shortcomings—the Gospel according to Luke should be the starting point.

In December of 1949 at the business session of the Society of Biblical Literature, Colwell announced the names of the members of the American editorial board, eighteen in all. Six members of the board were designated to form an executive committee, namely R. P. Casey,

K. W. Clark, E. C. Colwell (chairman), B. M. Metzger, M. M. Parvis (executive secretary), and A. P. Wikgren (vice-chairman).

At its first meeting, January 15 and 16, 1949, the executive committee took steps to organize a committee on Greek manuscripts of the New Testament, with Clark as chairman; a committee on the (early) versions of the New Testament, with Metzger as chairman; and a committee on patristic quotations from the New Testament, with Casey as chairman. At its meeting on April 30 and May 1, 1949, the executive committee organized a committee on Greek lectionaries, with Wikgren as chairman.

The next stage was to secure volunteers who would assist in collecting evidence from Greek manuscripts, from early versions, and from the Fathers. Dr. Colwell suggested to the committee that in the summer of 1950 I should be sent to Britain and the Continent in order to confer with scholars who might be interested and willing to collaborate in the project.

In consultation with my American colleagues it was decided that my first stop would be Oxford. Here I met with G. D. Kilpatrick and W. D. McHardy, both of whom showed interest in international collaboration. Leaving Oxford, my next stop was the University of Leeds, where I had lunch with Matthew Black who, as it turned out, was soon to return to teach in his native Scotland. Black's interest, like that of McHardy, was in the ancient Syriac versions (of which there are five including the *Diatessaron*).

A. M. Hunter of Aberdeen was next on my list. Since it was the summer holiday season, Hunter was not at his home in Aberdeen but, as I learned, was on a fishing trip in Galloway of Kirkcudbrightshire, in southwest Scotland. After a good many changes on minor railways I finally located him and had opportunity to acquaint him with the plans of the international project. It was natural that in the following years a warm friendship developed between myself and all four British scholars, each of whom subsequently visited our home in Princeton.

Although plans concerning the allocation of responsibility for the several versions could be only tentative, subject to change in the light of unforeseen exigencies, it was agreed that for the Gothic version I would get in touch with G. W. S. Friedrichsen, a British specialist in the Gothic language at that time resident in Washington, D.C. For the Old Church Slavonic version, Glanville Downey at Dumbarton Oaks in Washington and Professor Giuliano Bonfante at Princeton University appeared to be the most suitable. As for the Armenian version, it turned out that I was able to obtain the collaboration of Ralph Marcus of the University of Chicago and of Erroll F. Rhodes of the American Bible Society. Christopher Lash of England felt he could undertake only the first six chapters of the Ethiopic version of Luke. Eventually I obtained the help of Dr. Josef Hofmann, a pastor at Hofendorf, Niederbayern, who completed Luke for us.

British scholars were to be responsible for providing information from the Latin, Syriac, and Coptic versions. That left the Georgian version yet to be assigned. In view of the paucity of Western scholars who were competent in that language, our only hope appeared to be Canon Maurice Brière, honorary professor in the Institut Catholique de Paris. His name had been suggested by Robert P. Blake of Harvard, a member of the American committee on versions, and I had already been in correspondence with him in order to arrange for a mutually convenient time of meeting. Consequently, after leaving Britain, I travelled to Paris where I was able to confer with Brière. Happily he indicated that he would be willing to provide the information we needed.

Before I had left America, Dr. Colwell suggested that while in Europe I might well seek to contact two or three German scholars, in particular Erwin Nestle and Kurt Aland, in order to acquaint them with our plans concerning the project. Consequently, after leaving Paris I went to Ulm, where I found Erwin Nestle and his wife to be most hospitable to a stranger. Besides entertaining me at lunch in

Erwin Nestle

their home, Dr. Nestle took me to see the famous cathedral of Ulm, the tallest in Europe. We walked up to a suitable resting place in the tower and from there he pointed out various buildings below. Although Nestle was interested to learn about the project, he did not anticipate that he would be in a position to provide any material assistance. The work that he was then undertaking in the elaboration of the Nestle edition of the Greek New Testament, originally prepared by his father, Eberhard Nestle, took, he said, all of his time.

Before I left Nestle's home, he showed me an enormous heap of foolscap-size sheets lying on the dining-room table. These contained the handwritten Greek text of a synopsis or harmony of the four Gospels. Prepared several years before by Professor Paul W. Schmiedel of Zurich, this gigantic work was so extensive that no publisher would venture to issue it. As it turned out, two years after Nestle showed the harmony to me, Kurt Aland acquired access to the sheets, and, after shortening and adjusting the over-all scope, in 1963 he published Schmiedel's "Symphony of the Gospels," as he calls it in the preface, under the title *Synopsis Quattuor Evangeliorum.* Aland also added a new feature as an appendix, a threefold translation of the Coptic *Gospel of Thomas* (Latin, by G. Garitte; German, by E. Haenchen; English by B. M. Metzger).

From Ulm I went on to Switzerland in order to confer with Professor W. G. Kümmel, who for several years had been lecturing at the University of Zurich, and who in 1938 had contributed to *Theologische Rundschau* a discerning survey on "Textkritik und Textgeschichte des Neuen Testaments, 1914–1937." During a pleasant visit in his home, Kümmel told me that his interests had become more broadly focussed on New Testament history and theology and therefore, though expressing some interest in our project, he did not see his way clear to participate in it. Following this early acquaintance, for the next forty-five years until his death in 1995 he and I would exchange off-prints of articles as well as have occasional personal contact at meetings of learned societies or at his home in Marburg, where he was Bultmann's successor.

Following my conferences with Nestle and Kümmel, my visit with Kurt Aland had to be very brief. Since he was living in East Germany at Halle, he arranged to be at the Berlin Tempelhof airport at the time I was due to arrive there. We had an opportunity to talk together for several hours while seated in a restaurant at the airport; then I had to leave, for I had no visa to enter East Germany. Aland was, of course, interested to hear of the project, but thought we were making a mistake in using the Greek Textus Receptus as our collating base. I explained to him the reason we had selected it rather than a modern critical edition, which he preferred: we hoped to keep the apparatus within the bounds of a reasonable scope. Since the great majority of Greek manuscripts are late and agree with the Textus Receptus, they therefore would not need to be cited in the apparatus. On the other hand, if we used a modern critical edition as the basis for collation, the result would be the multiplication of pages containing citations of the least valuable manuscript evidence.

Before returning to the States from this, my first trip to Europe, I was planning to attend a performance of the Oberammergau Passion Play, to be given once again that year following a break in sequence caused by World War II. En route by train to Oberammergau I had a misadventure. At lunch time I inquired whether the restaurant coach would also be going to Oberammergau. I understood that it would, and so I left my assigned seat and took a leisurely meal in the restaurant coach. When, however, I wanted to return to my seat, I discovered that the train had been divided and that I was now travelling away from Oberammergau!

I looked around among the other passengers for someone to whom I might explain my predicament. A man with a kindly face told me not to worry; he was expecting to get off at the next station and would explain my situation to the stationmaster. This he did, and I was put on another train and told to make several *Umsteigen* until I reached a certain station to which my original train was headed. Meanwhile the stationmaster telephoned that station, giving information concerning my coach and seat number, so that my luggage could be taken off and held for me. Eventually I regained my luggage, topcoat, and hat, and even the copy of the magazine I had been reading. I arrived at Oberammergau much later that evening but was in time to attend the entire performance at the designated time the following day. I determined, however, that in the future I would endure the pangs of hunger rather than leave my assigned coach and seat.

The following year, after several meetings of the American executive committee, it was decided that, if feasible, a meeting should be arranged for the six members of the American committee to confer with the corresponding British members. Happily, Colwell was able to obtain funds from the Rockefeller Foundation in order to make such a combined meeting possible.

Early in June 1952 the members of the American committee embarked on the Cunard liner, the Queen Elizabeth. The five-day sea voyage enabled us to become still better acquainted with one another. Most of us began to call Dr. Colwell "Pomp," a nickname he had acquired in student days when he played the part of Pompey in a collegiate theatrical performance.

The meeting with our British counterparts was held in Oxford, with the noted papyrologist, Sir Harold I. Bell, serving as convener. The Americans stayed at the Randolph Hotel, and the sessions of the combined committees were held at Christ Church and Pembroke College Annex. Plans were laid for collating the manuscripts of Luke that Clark had microfilmed in 1950 for the Library of Congress at St. Catherine's Monastery, Mount Sinai. The British were to be responsible mainly for assembling the patristic material, along with evidence from several of the versions. The tentative plans laid during my trip in 1950 were discussed and generally agreed upon by the combined committees.

So started a collaborative project that took far longer to accomplish than any of us had anticipated at the beginning. Reports of progress were made each year at the text criticism seminar held in conjunction with the annual meetings of the Society of Biblical Literature. Similar annual reports were made by British members to the British Academy, which provided modest financial assistance.

In 1951, Colwell became vice president of his alma mater, Emory University, and consequently our executive committee would meet annually in the month of March at Atlanta, Georgia, amid the blooming azaleas for which that city is famous. Over the years more than two hundred North American scholars—many of them graduate students—provided collations of one or more Greek manuscripts. The collecting of patristic evidence proved to be more perplexing. Subsequent to 1950, when Casey moved to Great Britain, the following scholars served as chair of the American Committee on Patristic Quotations: P. Schubert, 1950–61; H. S. Murphy, 1961–62; M. J. Suggs, 1963–71; co-chair, 1972–73; G. D. Fee, co-chair, 1972–73; chairman 1973–.

In 1964 it was decided to draw up an experimental specimen of the apparatus in type. This specimen, covering Luke 20:1–6, was compiled jointly by Parvis for the American committee and by Dr. G. G. Willis, who had been appointed executive editor by the British committee. Printed by the Clarendon Press of Oxford, copies were circulated to some forty scholars for comments and criticism. In light of their responses various changes were made in the display and presentation of the textual variants.

Three years later Dr. Willis suffered an almost total loss of eyesight and resigned from his editorship. This was a serious setback, and it was not until 1970 that the British committee found a successor in Dr. J. Neville Birdsall of Birmingham University. Meanwhile the American committee appointed Kenneth Clark of Duke University as editor of the materials that had been compiled in America.

In 1972 the British Academy adopted the project as one of its research projects, and provided financial support for Birdsall during a period of "secondment" from his teaching post at Birmingham. Later, following Birdsall's resignation in 1978, Dr. J. Keith Elliott of Leeds University was appointed executive editor.

After the death of Colwell in 1974, I became chairman of the American executive committee and from time to time consulted with one or another of the British colleagues. My last trip in this capacity was in late September of 1984, when a three-day seminar on textual criticism of the Greek New Testament was to be held at Selwyn College, Cambridge. About twenty persons were invited, with Professor J. Martin Plumley of Cambridge serving as convener. One of the purposes of the seminar was to foster greater interest in textual criticism among younger scholars in Britain, and I was happy to make several new acquaintances.

Following the close of the seminar on the last afternoon and the departure of the others from Cripps Residence Hall, located across Grange Road from Selwyn, I remained alone at Cripps for one more night before flying back to the States the following day. I had earlier made arrangements for a taxi to pick me up early in the morning in order to take me to the bus terminal on Drummer Street in time for the coach leaving for Heathrow Airport. That morning I arose in good time and prepared to leave—only to discover that, since it was still the long vacation, no porter was present at that hour to unlock the gate. After briefly considering the feasibility of stacking chairs one on top of another in order to climb over the wall, I decided to investigate whether there might be some safer avenue of exit. After frantically scurrying here and there on the ground floor of Cripps Hall, I discovered that a door in the kitchen could be opened, and I stepped out into the lane that led to Grange Road. Then, in the darkness, with no illumination of street light, I stood awaiting the arrival of the taxi I had ordered the day before. No taxi arrived. I considered walking to Drummer Street, but the distance, the weight of my suitcase, and— most of all—the lack of time argued against attempting it. Finally, two headlights appeared in the darkness and I flagged down the approaching car. It proved to be a taxi that was going elsewhere to pick up a passenger. The driver, however, said that he was early and could therefore manage to take me to my bus and still have time for his customer. And this is what he did.

Thus ended my share in the lengthy period of gestation and development of the International Greek New Testament Project. Later in 1984, under the supervision of J. Keith Elliott of Leeds University as executive editor, Part One of *The Gospel according to Luke,* covering chapters 1–12, was published at Oxford by the Clarendon Press; it was followed in 1987 by Part Two, covering chapters 13–24.[1]

At the present time another committee of younger American and British scholars has begun work compiling a critical apparatus for the Gospel according to John.

---

[1]For another account of IGNTP, past and present, see Eldon Jay Epp's article, "The International Greek New Testament Project: Motivation and History," in the quarterly *Novum Testamentum* 39 (1997) 1–20.

Chapter 6

THE BIBLE SOCIETIES'
GREEK NEW TESTAMENT

AMONG important parachurch organizations that provide
assistance to members and congregations of all denominations are Bible societies. Noteworthy among such
institutions is the American Bible Society, organized in 1816
and located in New York City. Its board of managers
(called trustees since 1991) comprises both clergy and lay
members. Elected to the board in 1948, I was assigned to
serve on the subcommittee for translations, the secretary of
which was Dr. Eugene A. Nida. Trained in linguistics, Nida
was exactly suited to head the translation department of
the Bible Society. Intelligent, energetic, and far-seeing, he
planned for the production of translations into languages
that hitherto had no biblical book available, as well as
arranged for the revision of earlier renderings that needed
reexamination.

In the early months of 1954 Dr. Nida got in touch with
me about another type of project that was related to the
work of Bible translators. This was a proposal that the Bible
Society sponsor the preparation of an edition of the Greek
New Testament with an apparatus suited to the needs of
translators and students. Since it had always proved wise to
have, whenever possible, a committee rather than only one
person produce a new translation, Nida reasoned that an
edition of the basic Greek text would also profit from being
prepared by a committee. It is remarkable that over the
generations, all editions of the Greek New Testament, with

one exception, had been produced by a single individual; the exception was the edition published in 1881 by two British scholars, Westcott and Hort, whose background and training were more or less similar. Nida suggested that an international committee should be formed in order to secure the text-critical insights of several scholars of diverse training and backgrounds. My response to Nida's proposal was a hearty acquiescence.

The committee for the Bible Societies' *Greek New Testament.*
From right to left: C. M. Martini, K. Aland, A. Wikgren,
B. M. Metzger, and M. Black (with K. Junack, Aland's assistant)

In subsequent correspondence Nida invited me to serve on such a committee and requested that I suggest the names of three or four other scholars who had made contributions to New Testament textual studies and who might participate on such an international committee. After some consideration I proposed the names of Allen Wikgren of Chicago, Matthew Black of Scotland, Kurt Aland of Münster in West Germany, and Arthur Vööbus, originally from Estonia but more recently, after Russia had invaded that country, at Maywood Lutheran Theological Seminary in

Illinois. Nida interviewed all of them and happily obtained the agreement of each to serve on the committee.

It might be wondered why G. D. Kilpatrick of Oxford was not invited to participate. Actually, Nida had conferred with him as well as with Wilfred J. Bradnock, secretary of the British and Foreign Bible Society, and learned that the BFBS had already arranged for Kilpatrick to undertake a limited revision of the 1904 edition of the Nestle Greek New Testament and to provide a selected apparatus of variant readings. Neither Bradnock nor Kilpatrick thought it would be wise to defer that project or to put additional responsibilities on Kilpatrick.

By 1955 the National Bible Society of Scotland and the Württemberg Bible Society of Germany agreed to join the American Bible Society in sponsoring the production of the new edition. The three societies were joined later by the Netherlands Bible Society and by the British and Foreign Bible Society.

The committee of five scholars mentioned above carried out its work in four principal stages: (1) On the basis of Westcott and Hort's edition of the Greek New Testament, a comparison was made of the text and apparatus of several other editions, including those of Nestle, Bover, Merk, and Vogels, and to some extent those of Tischendorf and von Soden, in order to determine which of the variant readings warranted further study; (2) data on several thousand sets of variants were gathered, not only from printed editions, commentaries, and technical studies, but also from hitherto unused papyri, uncials, minuscules, and lectionaries; (3) about six hundred variations in punctuation, which appeared to merit consideration, were selected and compared in editions of the Greek text and in the principal English, German, and French translations; and finally, (4) the Greek text was established, the degree of certainty for the reading adopted in the text was estimated, and a decision was made whether or not to include a set of variant readings in the apparatus.

The collection of the masses of detailed information involved in stages (1) and (2) was accomplished by J. Harold

Greenlee and Robert P. Markham, assisted by Karen Munson and the staff of the Institute for New Testament Textual Research at Münster. The punctuation apparatus was prepared by J. Harold Greenlee, Robert P. Markham, and Harold K. Moulton.

Over a period of ten years the members of the committee met annually for five weeks during the summer vacation period. Happily, arrangements were made for our families to be with us, and consequently, lasting friendships developed not only among the adults but among the children as well. Three of these meetings were held in Europe at St. Andrews (in 1959), Utrecht (1961), and Cambridge (1963), where we were guests of the Bible societies that had joined with the American Society. During the meeting held in Cambridge the committee was given permission by the university library to consult an important bilingual manuscript, Codex Bezae, in order to resolve several disputed palaeographical points. The other seven meetings were held at various places in New England, either near the seacoast or by a lake.

After the first four years Vööbus felt that the press of other duties prevented him from further participation in the project. Without his presence, however, it would happen, of course, that occasionally the vote on a problem was two against two. In such cases we would lay aside the matter, to be taken up again the following year.

Throughout the years of the committee's activity each member brought his own special expertise to the common task. The discussions were lively and often exhilarating. Finally, after spending virtually a year of our lives in company with one another, the result of our labor was set up in type by the Maurice Jacobs firm in Philadelphia (at that time the printer of the *Journal of Biblical Literature*) and a copy sent to the Bible Society in Stuttgart for printing. When, after some months, nothing had happened, investigation disclosed that the copy had gone astray in the mails. Another copy was prepared and taken personally by Mr. Jacobs to Stuttgart. In 1966 copies of the completed book were published in New York, London, Edinburgh, Amsterdam, and Stuttgart by each of the five Bible Societies.

A second edition appeared in 1968. This incorporated a number of typographical corrections, forty-five changes in the evaluation of the evidence (i.e., changes in the ratings of A, B, C, and D), eleven alterations involving brackets, and five modifications of text or apparatus. For the preparation of the second (and subsequent) editions, the committee had been enlarged by the addition of Carlo M. Martini of the Pontifical Biblical Institute in Rome.

A third edition, published in 1975, incorporated a thorough revision of the Greek text. In a series of sessions held in 1969 at Freudenstadt in Germany, the committee considered not only a number of suggestions made by specialists in the field of New Testament studies, but also numerous recommendations resulting from the experience of the members of the committee as they worked with the text of the earlier editions. As a result of these discussions, more than five hundred changes were introduced into the third edition.

Correlated to the text of the third edition is a companion volume entitled *A Textual Commentary on the Greek New Testament*,[1] edited by the present writer on behalf of the committee. This volume sets forth an account of the considerations that led the committee to make its decisions for each of the fourteen hundred sets of variant readings included in the apparatus. The *Commentary* also gives attention to about six hundred additional textual problems, most of them in the book of Acts.

In 1981 Dr. Nida once again called together the committee to make decisions in the preparation of a fourth edition. The composition of the committee, which met for two weeks at Freudenstadt, was somewhat different this time. In accordance with the understanding from the beginning of the project, when a member of the committee was retired from his academic post, he would also be retired

---

[1] New York: United Bible Societies, 1971.

Examining leaves of Codex Vaticanus at the Vatican library

from the committee. This meant that, in 1981, neither Black nor Wikgren met with us, being replaced by two new members, Barbara Aland of Münster and Johannes Karavidopoulos of Thessaloniki.

Following the committee meeting in Germany I went on to Rome in order to attend the annual meeting of the International Society of New Testament Studies. During the sessions arrangements were made to visit the Vatican Library, where I wished to consult certain pages of the celebrated fourth-century Codex Vaticanus, a photograph of which was to be included in my book *Manuscripts of the Greek Bible.*[2] The margin opposite the text of Hebrews 1:3 contains a curiously indignant note added by a thirteenth-century corrector who restored the original (but erroneous) reading of the manuscript (φανερῶν), for which an earlier corrector had substituted the correct reading (φέρων). The note reads "Fool and knave, can't you leave the old reading alone, and not alter it!"

---

[2] *Manuscripts of the Greek Bible: An Introduction to Greek Palaeography* (New York: Oxford University Press, 1981).

The results of the decisions taken by the committee in 1981 were not issued until 1993, when the fourth edition of *The Greek New Testament* was published by the Deutsche Bibelgesellschaft and by the United Bible Societies. One reason for the long delay was the time required for the work (undertaken by the institute at Münster) of selection, collation, and multiple checking of the various groups of witnesses—Greek, versional, and patristic. The text of the edition remained unchanged, but 284 additional sets of variant readings were added in the apparatus, and in place of the punctuation apparatus a discourse segmentation apparatus was prepared by Roger Omanson, a translation consultant of the United Bible Societies. On the negative side was the elimination, for some unexplained reason, of evidence of the Gothic version, made by Ulfilas about AD 385. Likewise, the computer-generated Greek characters used for the text and apparatus are, in the judgment of many users, less attractive and harder to read than the beautiful Porson font of Greek type that I had recommended for the earlier editions. In the following year the second edition of my *Textual Commentary,* which incorporated discussions concerning the additional sets of variant readings, was published.[3]

Over the years, the United Bible Societies' edition of the Greek New Testament has been widely adopted as the basis for translations and revisions of earlier vernacular renderings in many countries and cultures. The influence of its text was spread even more widely when, in 1979 and with the permission of the United Bible Societies, the Nestle-Aland edition replaced the Nestle Greek text with the UBS

---

[3]*A Textual Commentary on the Greek New Testament* (2d ed.; Stuttgart: United Bible Societies, 1994). Through an unfortunate oversight the discussion of Romans 9:5 was not adjusted to reflect the change introduced into the UBS Greek text (a comma instead of the earlier colon). Consequently the reader will be nonplussed in attempting to make sense of the disparity between lemma and discussion. In a subsequent printing the discussion is to be rectified.

Greek text, leaving only the apparatus to continue the Nestle tradition.

During the past few years the need to explain the making and the use of the Bible Societies' *Greek New Testament* has taken me twice to Russia. With the opening of the former Soviet Union to Western cultural and political influences, the United Bible Societies arranged for international workshops to be held on the subject of "Bible Text and Bible Translation." Assisted by the Patriarchal and Synodal Commission of the Russian Orthodox Church and the newly reestablished Russian Bible Society, in September of 1992 a two-week workshop in Moscow was arranged through Dr. Manuel M. Jinbachian of Strasbourg. About forty persons were present, some from distant lands of the former Soviet Union, all of them interested in Bible translating. Dr. Paul Ellingworth of Scotland, Dr. John Callow and David Clark of England, and Dr. Jinbachian gave lectures on the theory and practice of translation, while I presented information about the transmission of the Greek text of the New Testament and the need to evaluate variant readings attested by the earliest manuscript copies. Dr. Anatoly A. Alexeev and Dr. Serge Ovsiannikov gave lectures concerning different types of translation in the Church Slavonic tradition. By means of headphones and simultaneous translation, each participant heard in his or her native English or Russian what was being said at the moment. The sessions were held in Hotel Rossiya, located near Red Square and the Kremlin and reputed to be the largest hotel in the world, able to accommodate six thousand guests.

The following year a similar workshop was held at St. Petersburg, with about twenty-five translators present. The sessions were held in St. Petersburg Theological Academy, a twenty-minute walk from Hotel Moscow where we had our accommodations. Dr. Jinbachian asked me to make a similar presentation to this group as at the previous year's workshop. Other participants included Mr. Martin Hoegger of the Swiss Bible Society, Dr. Simon Crisp of England, Dr.

Krijn van der Jagt of Nairobi, and Dr. Howard Clark Kee of Philadelphia.

At both seminars there was a readiness to undertake translation or revision, as the case might be, as well as recognition of the need to adopt a style of rendering that takes into account linguistic and cultural features of the target language. There was, however, some resistance among ecclesiastical authorities to the idea of replacing the traditional Byzantine Textus Receptus with an earlier text as witnessed by Greek papyri and early uncial manuscripts. On my second visit I had the opportunity to present a lecture through an interpreter to the faculty of the St. Petersburg Theological Academy on the transmission of the Greek text of the New Testament. To what extent what I presented concerning the development and evaluation of the Byzantine form of text was persuasive, I do not know.

Chapter 7

TRANSLATING THE BIBLE:
THE REVISED STANDARD VERSION

THE word "standard" in the name of the Revised Standard Version of the Bible came to be adopted in the following way. Toward the latter part of the nineteenth century a revision of the so-called Authorized or King James Version of 1611 was undertaken by a committee of biblical scholars in Great Britain that formed in 1870. Soon after the organization of the British committee, an invitation was extended to American scholars to cooperate with them in this work of common interest.

For ten years the two groups worked separately in accord with the following arrangement. The British revisers would send confidentially their revision at various stages to the American revisers. All the American suggestions were given special consideration by the British committee prior to the publication of the New Testament in 1881 and the Old Testament in 1885. Subsequently the Americans were allowed to present, in an appendix to the Revised Version, all the remaining differences of reading and rendering of importance that the British committee had declined to adopt. On the other hand, the American committee agreed not to issue an edition of their own, embodying their preferences that had not been adopted, for a period of fourteen years.

After the expiration of that period, in 1901 the American Revised Version of the Bible was published in New York by Thomas Nelson and Sons and copyrighted to protect the text from unauthorized changes. The version was designated the American Standard Version, with the acronym ASV. In 1928 the copyright was transferred to the International Council of Religious Education, a body in which the educational boards of forty of the major Protestant denominations of the United States and Canada were associated. In 1929, the body appointed the Standard Bible Committee of fifteen scholars to have charge of the text and authorized them to undertake further revision if it was deemed necessary. The chairman of the committee was Dr. Luther A. Weigle, dean of Yale Divinity School, and the vice-chairman was Professor William Park Armstrong of Princeton Theological Seminary.

The work of the Standard Bible Committee was begun in 1930; it was suspended in 1932 because of the lack of funds for members' travel and accommodations expenses (unlike other Bible translation committees, individual members of the RSV committee received no financial compensation for their work). In 1937 the necessary budget was provided, and the revision proceeded. Seven more members were added to the committee, which worked in two sections, one for the Old Testament and one for the New. A decade later, on February 11, 1946, the Revised Standard Version of the New Testament was published by Thomas Nelson and Sons. Six years later, on September 30, 1952 (September 30 is the festal day of St. Jerome, the translator of the Latin Vulgate Bible), the Old Testament was published.

The new version was launched with an unprecedented publicity campaign. On the evening of the day of publication, in the United States, in Canada, and in many other places, 3,418 community observances were held with more than one and a half million persons attending.

The fanfare, however, did not protect the new version from criticism. Unfounded and malicious accusations were brought against several members of the committee, alleging that they were either Communists or Communist sympathizers—allegations that, at the insistence of Senator Joseph McCarthy of Wisconsin, were eventually printed in the official United States Air Force Training Manual.

Finally, after a thorough investigation conducted by non-partisan authorities, these entirely unsupported charges were rebutted as "venomous nonsense" on the floor of the House of Representatives in Washington and the edition of the manual in question was withdrawn.[1]

Meanwhile, a pastor of a church in Rocky Mount, North Carolina, publically burned with a blowtorch a copy of what he termed "a heretical, communist-inspired Bible." The ashes were put in a metal box and sent to Dean Weigle at Yale Divinity School, who had served as convener of the

Ashes of a copy of the Revised Standard Version Bible (1952)

---

[1] *The Congressional Record,* 86th Cong., 2d sess., 1960, 106, pt. 3: 3505–7; pt. 5: 6872–74; pt. 6: 8247–84.

Standard Bible Committee. That box, with its contents, is now among the Bible committee's collection of books and archives, a reminder that, though in previous centuries Bible translators were sometimes burned, today happily it is only a copy of the translation that meets such a fate.

Shortly after the publication of the entire Bible a request came from the General Convention of the Protestant Episcopal Church that a revision of the English translation of the books of the Apocrypha be undertaken. In response, the Division of Christian Education of the National Council of the Churches of Christ in the U.S.A. (into which the International Council of Religious Education had merged) organized a small committee to work with Dean Weigle in making a translation of these books also. Among the scholars accepting this assignment were four members who had served on the earlier committee, namely, Millar Burrows, Yale University; Henry J. Cadbury, Harvard University; Clarence T. Craig, Drew Theological Seminary; and Frederick C. Grant, Union Theological Seminary. To these were added four new members, Floyd V. Filson, McCormick Theological Seminary; Robert H. Pfeiffer, Harvard University; Allen P. Wikgren, University of Chicago; and myself. As the youngest member of the committee, I was appointed secretary. Following the death of Craig (August 20, 1954), J. Carter Swaim, Western Theological Seminary, Pittsburgh, was added to the membership of the committee.

The work of the committee involved the preparation and circulation of mimeographed drafts of translation, the discussion and resolution of all disputed points in face-to-face conference, the circulation of new drafts embodying the decisions reached in conference, and a final review of each book in the light of written agenda proposed by members of the committee and of an advisory board made up of representatives appointed by denominations that accepted the invitation to review the drafts.

During the next four years meetings of the committee were held at Yale Divinity School and at Northfield Inn in East Northfield, Massachusetts. At East Northfield we stayed and worked in a building called the Chateau, which belonged to the inn. The Chateau contained, it was said, ninety-nine rooms and had been built in the previous century as the private residence of a millionaire. After his death the Chateau was acquired by the inn so as to accommodate additional guests. Each time our committee met, however, very few other guests resided in the Chateau, so we more or less had it to ourselves.

Our committee of nine members soon developed a fine esprit de corps, and the two-week sessions seemed to me to go by rapidly. At our meals, which were taken in the dining room of the inn, there was, of course, opportunity for repartee and the exchanging of stories. Weigle had a store of Pennsylvania Dutch stories and Wikgren contributed jokes that he recollected from a Danish book of humor. Pfeiffer was by nature especially appreciative of funny stories and would react with uproarious laughter. After some days the headwaiter moved us to an alcove on the porch of the inn, where our frequent outbursts of laughter would not disturb the sober decorum that the other guests obviously preferred.

Early in the course of our work of translating, Dean Weigle, thinking that many Protestants would welcome some information concerning the books of the Apocrypha, suggested that I draw up a popular account of their origin and influence. This suggestion appealed to me, and consequently in 1957, the same year that Thomas Nelson and Sons issued the Revised Standard Version Apocrypha, my volume *An Introduction to the Apocrypha* was published.[2]

A year or two later, Wilbur D. Ruggels, vice-president and editor of religious books at Oxford University Press in New York, invited Herbert G. May, the professor of Old Testament at Oberlin College, and me to edit a study edition of the Bible, based on the Revised Standard Version. Published in 1962, *The Oxford Annotated Bible* immediately gained wide use, especially among ministers and students in

---

[2]New York: Oxford University Press.

colleges, universities, and theological seminaries. The volume was followed in 1965 by *The Oxford Annotated Apocrypha,* and later that same year the two were published together as *The Oxford Annotated Bible, with the Apocrypha.*

Because of the growing acceptance of this study Bible in Catholic circles, the Press decided to approach Cardinal Cushing, archbishop of Boston, for his formal approval of the edition. He expressed his willingness to consider the request if a joint committee of Catholic and Protestant scholars reviewed the matter and made recommendations. Thereupon a committee was formed, consisting of Professor Philip J. King, St. John's Seminary, Boston, and Professor W. Van Etten Casey, S.J., Holy Cross College, Worcester, Massachusetts, who, together with Professor Eugene H. Maly, Mount St. Mary's Academy of the West, Norwood, Ohio, consulted with May and myself.

This informal committee reached full agreement on all details. It was decided that no changes were desirable or necessary in the text or the footnotes of the Revised Standard Version or in the general or special introductory articles except for that upon Ecclesiastes. A few minor changes were made in some of the annotations. These consisted chiefly in adding a brief explanation to particular phrases or verses to indicate where Catholic interpretation differs from Protestant interpretation.

Two weeks after the committee submitted its recommendations, Cardinal Cushing granted his endorsement in the form of an *imprimatur* to *The Oxford Annotated Bible, with the Apocrypha.* He also expressed his "pleasure to be associated with this ecumenical venture which should have far-reaching fruitful results."

A further development took place in Great Britain, where Collins Publishers of Glasgow responded to the ecumenical concerns of contemporary Christianity. At the initiative of the Catholic Biblical Association of Great Britain, and with Catholic ecclesiastical approval, and by agreement with the Standard Bible Committee and the National Council of Churches, Collins issued the Catholic edition of the Revised Standard Version of the Bible (1966). In it the Deuterocanonical books were placed among the books of the Old Testament in the order followed in the Latin Vulgate. An important feature of the Catholic edition is the acceptance of the common English spelling of biblical names instead of that based on the Latin Vulgate, which had previously been the practice in Catholic Bibles.

Owing to his advanced age, in 1966 Dean Weigle requested that he become honorary chairman of the Standard Bible Committee, and Herbert May took Weigle's place as chairman of the committee (with myself as vice-chairman). This arrangement continued until May's tragic death in an automobile accident on October 6, 1977, after which I became chairman of the committee.

Meanwhile the advisability of issuing a second edition of the Revised Standard Version of the New Testament was being considered. Since the New Testament was first issued in 1946, proposals for modification had been submitted to the committee by individuals and by two denominational committees. All of these were given careful attention by the Standard Bible Committee. The decision that it was appropriate to produce a second edition was not made until after the United Bible Societies published a new edition of *The Greek New Testament* in 1966. Making use of this edition and consulting linguistic studies that had been published since 1946, the Standard Bible Committee introduced a limited number of significant changes in the RSV New Testament and issued a second edition in 1971. Two passages, the long ending of Mark (16:9–20) and the account of the woman caught in adultery (John 7:53–8:11), were lifted from the footnotes and restored to the text, separated from it by a blank space and accompanied by informative notes describing the various arrangements of the text in the ancient authorities.

In light of new manuscript support a number of other changes were also introduced throughout. Some of the revisions clarified the meaning through rephrasing or reordering the text. Even when the changes appeared to be largely matters of English style, they had the purpose of presenting to the reader more adequately the meaning of the text. For example, the traditional rendering of Luke 17:34 was changed in order to conform to the Greek text. Instead of "I tell you, in that night there shall be two men in one bed; the one shall be taken, and the other shall be left," the committee decided that there was no reason to retain the word "men," which, contrary to all preceding English translations, the King James translators had inserted without warrant from the Greek text.

Since among many Christian groups there was an increasing interest in the Apocrypha, the Vatican secretariat for Christian unity together with the United Bible Societies drew up guiding principles for the production of interconfessional translations. At the suggestion of Lady Priscilla and Sir William Collins, it was proposed that the Collins publishing house should issue an edition of the Revised Standard Version as a "common Bible." Under the leadership of Dr. Reginald C. Fuller, chairman of the Catholic Bible Association of Great Britain, and Dom Bernard Orchard, O.S.B., general secretary of the World Catholic Federation for the Biblical Apostolate, a plan was evolved to divide the books of the Apocrypha into two sections, those that the Catholic Church regards as Deuterocanonical and those that are not so regarded. The Apocryphal/Deuterocanonical books were placed between the testaments, as is normally done in Protestant Bibles, but 1 and 2 Esdras and the Prayer of Manasseh were transferred to the end of the Deuterocanonicals, separated from them by a blank page and accompanied by a note explaining that the Catholic Church does not accept them as canonical. Thus, for the first time, a clear distinction was made that would commend itself to the different Christian churches.

It should be noted that in such an arrangement Catholics made a significant departure from the accepted practice in their long history. The separation of the Deuterocanonical books from their place throughout the Old Testament is

An audience with Pope Paul VI

essentially an accommodation to the Protestant arrangement of the books of the Bible.

In 1973, shortly after the Collins publishing house, joined by Thomas Nelson and Sons in the United States, had issued its *Common Bible,* Lady Priscilla Collins, a convert to Catholicism, arranged to present a specially bound copy to Pope Paul VI at the Vatican. Consequently, on May 9th of that year the pope granted a private audience to Lady Priscilla and Sir William Collins, joined by Herbert May and myself. A fifth person included in the group was the Greek Orthodox archbishop Athenagoras of Thyateira and Great Britain, exarch of the ecumenical patriarchate of Constantinople, who had earlier endorsed this ecumenical edition.

During our audience with the pope, his Holiness spoke briefly in English to each of us; this was followed by his reading a statement in Italian, translated into English by a priest from San Francisco. When we were leaving the Vatican, Archbishop Athenagoras spoke to me to the effect that, worthy as *The Common Bible* might be, it failed to live up to its name, for it lacked the full canon of books recognized as authoritative by Eastern Orthodox Churches. The Greek, the Russian, the Ukrainian, the Bulgarian, the Serbian, the Armenian, and other Eastern churches accept not only the traditional Deuterocanonical books that are received by the Roman Catholic Church, but also the Third Book of Maccabees. Furthermore, in Greek Bibles Psalm 151 stands at the close of the Psalter, and the Fourth Book of Maccabees is printed as an appendix to the Old Testament. Inasmuch as these texts were not included in the *Common Bible* presented to Pope Paul, Archbishop Athenagoras expressed to me the hope that steps might be taken to produce a truly ecumenical edition of the Holy Scriptures.

Actually, in 1972 a subcommittee of the Standard Bible Translation Committee had already been commissioned to prepare a translation of 3 and 4 Maccabees and Psalm 151. The members of the subcommittee were Demetrios J. Constantelos, Stockton State College, Pomona, New Jersey; Sherman E. Johnson, Church Divinity School of the Pacific, Berkeley, California; Robert A. Kraft, University of Pennsylvania; Allen Wikgren; and myself. In 1976 the completed translation of the three texts was made available to the five publishers licensed to issue the RSV Bible. Oxford University Press immediately took steps to include the additional texts in *The Oxford Annotated Bible, with the Apocrypha.*

This enlarged edition was published by the Oxford University Press on May 19, 1977, under the title, *The New Oxford Annotated Bible, with the Apocrypha,* Expanded Edition. Later that year arrangements were made for me to present on December 18 a copy to his All Holiness, Demetrios I, the ecumenical patriarch of Constantinople and titular head of the several Orthodox Churches. The protocol of making the presentation was worked out through the good offices of Professor Vasil Istavridis of Istanbul, who had received a doctorate in theology at Boston University and who served as my interpreter during the presentation. In accepting the gift, the ecumenical patriarch expressed his satisfaction at the availability of an edition of the sacred

Presentation of a copy of the first truly ecumenical edition of the
Bible in English to the ecumenical patriarch, Demetrios I

Scriptures that English readers belonging to all of the main branches of the Christian church could use.

The story of the making of the Revised Standard Version of the Bible with the expanded Apocryphal/ Deuterocanonical books covers twenty-five years (1952–77). It is an account of the slow but steady triumph of ecumenical concern over more limited sectarian interests. For the first time since the Reformation, one edition of the Bible received the blessings of leaders of the Protestant, Roman Catholic, and Eastern Orthodox churches alike.

Before continuing the saga of the development of the Revised Standard Version, I may perhaps mention several happenings during my trip to Istanbul. En route I stopped at Cairo to attend the First International Conference of Coptic Studies held in that city. During the conference my roommate at the Shepheard Hotel in Cairo was my long-time friend, Robert McLachlan Wilson of St. Mary's College, St. Andrews, Scotland. Since there were only two flights a week from Cairo to Istanbul, I had made arrangements to leave one day earlier than the close of the conference. The evening previous to my departure I paid my bill at the hotel and arranged for a taxi to call for me the next morning. So that the hotel would not charge Wilson for my accommodations, before retiring I gave him the receipt of my payment.

The next morning at the appointed time, and without wakening Wilson, I went downstairs to the taxi and prepared to leave the hotel, carrying my luggage. A watcher at the door, noticing that I had not stopped at the cashier's desk, challenged me as a thief leaving without settling my account. I explained that I had paid the night before, whereupon he asked to see my receipt. Of course I could not show it to him, nor did it seem feasible to go back in order to retrieve it—for, owing to Wilson's severely impaired hearing, even though I would knock on the door of our room, it was unlikely that I would be able to arouse him. Furthermore, I did not want to delay too long lest I miss my departing plane.

It seemed best to disregard the accusation that I was a thief, and so I put my luggage into the trunk of the taxi. But the man increased his shouting to such a degree that I felt I really had to return to the hotel—but now the thought entered my mind, what if the taxi driver should drive away with my luggage! Fortunately, however, the driver returned with me into the hotel, and still more fortunately, the same person was at the cashier's desk as on the previous evening. He remembered that I had paid my bill, and so was able to vouch that I was not a thief.

After arriving at the airport at Istanbul and having completed customs formalities, I proceeded to change money into the local currency. Then I went out to find a taxi to take me to my hotel. As the taxi began to drive away I noticed that someone had come out of the booth where I had changed money, and he was waving a parcel in the air. It was the copy of the Bible that I intended to give to the ecumenical patriarch! Throughout my entire trip I had not packed the parcel in my luggage, lest it go astray en route, but had always carried it with me. Now, however, I had absentmindedly left it lying on the cashier's counter, where an honest bystander noticed my oversight. My great gratitude was scarcely measured by the gratuity I gave him in exchange for the parcel, without which my visit the next day at the Phanar (the patriarch's official residence) would have been both pointless and exceedingly embarrassing.

Chapter 8

Translating the Bible:
The New Revised Standard Version

Several years before the untimely death of Herbert
May in 1977 (mentioned earlier, p. 82) the Standard
Bible Committee had given serious consideration to
the need for and advisability of undertaking a revision of
the Revised Standard Version of the Old Testament. In
view of the increasing numbers of ancient Hebrew scrolls
and fragments that had been discovered in the Dead Sea
area, as well as the availability of various texts in related
Semitic languages from which new insights could be gained
concerning Hebrew lexicography, the time seemed to be
appropriate to begin a full revision of the Old Testament,
and to complete the limited revision of the New Testament
that had been issued in 1971.

Consequently, in 1974 the National Council of Churches
directed that a thorough revision of the RSV be undertaken in accordance with the following mandates. Necessary changes were to be made (1) in paragraph structure
and punctuation; (2) in the elimination of archaisms while
retaining the flavor of the Tyndale–King James Bible tradition; (3) in attaining greater accuracy, clarity, and euphony;
and (4) in eliminating masculine-oriented language concerning people, so far as this could be done without distort-
ing passages that reflect the historical situation of ancient
patriarchal culture and society.

Thereafter the Standard Bible Committee was convened twice every year, usually one week in January and

Members of the New Revised Standard Version Bible Committee,
June 1981 (with two Princeton Seminary graduate students who
served as recording secretaries). Front row from left: Lucetta Mowry,
Walter Harrelson, William Beardslee, Bruce Metzger, Charles
Myers, Jr. (student), Robert Dentan. Middle Row: Bruce Vawter, C.M.,
Allen Wikgren, Reginald H. Fuller, George MacRae, S.J.,
Harry Orlinsky, Delbert Hillers, Demetrios Constantelos. Top row:
Paul Minear, James Sanders, William Holladay, Alfred Sauer,
Jimmy Roberts, Marvin Pope, Charles Cosgrove (student)

one week in June. Eventually several additional members
were added to the Old Testament section (making a total of
twenty members) so that three subsections could meet simultaneously and thus keep up with the panels that were
working on the New Testament and on the books of the
Apocrypha. Robert Dentan and Walter Harrelson, along
with one other member of the Old Testament section, served
as conveners of the three Old Testament subsections, and I
served in that capacity for the New Testament section and for
the section for the Apocrypha, which met in alternate seasons.

In the course of discussing the several proposals for
change, it is understandable that occasionally sharp differences of opinion would be expressed. What might appear

to one person to be a matter of relatively minor importance might appear to another to be of major significance. Among problems of finding a satisfactory rendering (or, in some cases, the least unsatisfactory rendering), I recall several that were debated more than once. One such question concerned the best way to translate the Hebrew word *miknas*, which refers to part of the high priest's linen garments. Traditionally this word had been rendered "breeches," but since the garment is said to extend from the hips to the thighs (Exodus 28:42), that rendering seemed to be inappropriate. But what is more suitable? One of the older members of the committee declared, "Why, of course, drawers is what is meant." Younger members proposed "shorts" or even "skivvies." Still others favored "pants" or "underpants." Eventually the somewhat cumbersome word "undergarments" was chosen.

In the New Testament a recurring problem arose concerning the appropriate rendering of the Greek word *doulos*. Defined by classical Greek lexicons as "slave," this translation is certainly correct in many places in the New Testament, and several members of the committee preferred to use this rendering everywhere. But other members were impressed by the fact that in the Greek translation of the Old Testament *doulos* frequently renders the Hebrew *ᶜebed*, a word variously translated "servant," "slave," "official," "bondman." Therefore, despite vigorous debates that were renewed more than once in the New Testament committee, a majority voted to retain the traditional rendering in such passages as, "Paul, a servant of Jesus Christ" (Romans 1:1), "the song of Moses, the servant of God" (Revelation 15:3), and "Praise our God, all you his servants" (Revelation 19:5). In these passages a footnote now informs the reader that the Greek is literally "slave" or "slaves."

Occasionally a change was adopted that at a later session appeared to be ill-advised. Such was a proposal that I made one day in the interest of uniformity, namely, that the Greek name *Ioudas* should be rendered throughout the New Testament by "Judas," including its occurrence in the title and in the first verse of the Letter of Jude. That night, however, I began to consider how perplexed readers would be to find in their New Testament a letter of Judas! The next morning, therefore, I reopened the discussion and was able to persuade a majority of the committee that the wisest course was to retain the traditional rendering for the Letter of Jude and to use a footnote indicating that the Greek reads *Judas*.[1]

It will not be surprising to those who have worked in similar committees that not all our debate was conducted with serious decorum. Occasionally the progress of the discussion led to levity as one suggestion or another might strike a humorous chord. Such occurred, for example, in discussing the meaning of *eisedu* in 1 Maccabees 6:46, which describes the bravery of a Jewish freedom-fighter who, taking a sword, managed to come close to the leading elephant in the phalanx of the Syrian army; then "he ——— the elephant, stabbed it from beneath, and killed it; but it fell to the ground upon him and there he died." In seeking for a suitable word to translate the Greek verb, first one then another member proposed various renderings, such as "went to," "stooped under," "slid beneath," and a variety of other verbs, ending with "he snuck under the elephant"! By this time everyone was laughing. Finally it was decided to use the rather colorless "he got under the elephant."

On one occasion the afternoon discussion in the New Testament section was prolonged beyond the time for the evening meal (working days normally ran from 9:00 A.M. to 9:00 P.M.). On this day the Princeton Seminary library, including the room in which the New Testament group was working, was to be closed at 5:00 P.M. Neither I as chair nor the other members had been paying attention to the passing of time, and when we finally broke off for the evening

---

[1] Among earlier English renderings of the Bible, Wycliffe (1380) and Tyndale (1534) used Judas (Iudas) in the title of the epistle; Moffatt (1913) used Judas, followed by Jude in parentheses. Of course, in German, Dutch, Swedish, Spanish, and other European languages, no such distinction is made.

meal we found that the janitor had locked all doors leading out of the library. We finally discovered that one window in our workroom could be opened, and so, after I had placed a chair outside on the ground, all of us climbed out, one-by-one. Fortunately the place of our meeting was on the ground floor.

After the Old and New Testament sections of the committee had completed their assignments, the results were turned over to two editorial committees for necessary smoothing and standardizing of work that had extended over a span of about sixteen years. During those years a certain dynamic had evolved, which meant that adjustments needed to be made in each Testament. This editorial work was accomplished for the Old Testament and the Apocrypha by a committee comprising Robert Dentan, Walter Harrelson, and myself, working a total of seventy-six days, and for the New Testament by Paul Minear, Lucetta Mowry, and myself, working a total of thirty-three days.

Finally, two additional tasks fell on my shoulders. One was the introduction of a limited number of adjustments within and between the Old and New Testaments. The other was more extensive. Both editorial committees had agreed to my suggestion that, in the interest of improving euphony, the number of occurrences of the word "which" might well be decreased. A few instances of the word, which occurs more than 4,500 times in the Old and New Testaments of the King James Version, had indeed been attended to in the Revised Standard Version of 1952—notably when the reference was to a person (as "Our Father which art in heaven"). But a very great many more instances remained, and some of these I thought could be replaced with "that," thereby reducing unpleasant hissing sounds when the version is read aloud. Of course, when following a comma or a preposition "which" must be retained, and this accounts for most of the 1,284 instances that were kept in this revision of the RSV.

Near the close of the work of the entire committee, we gave attention to the question of what we should call the revision. In seeking a suitable designation for the updated form of the Revised Standard Version, two considerations needed to be balanced: (1) The name ought to indicate some continuity with the previous form of the version; (2) at the same time the name ought to be distinctive and not easily confused with other existing English versions.

In accordance with the former consideration it was thought necessary to retain the word "Standard." Possible designations, accordingly, were "Ecumenical Standard Version" and "New Standard Version." It was also suggested that "Revised Standard Version" be retained, followed by a designation such as "New Edition," or "1990 Edition," or "Final Edition."

Another possibility was to use "Revised Standard Version" with a prefix; among those that we were considered were "New," "Second," and "Improved." Of course, we needed also to take into account the acronym that would be formed from whatever name was chosen—and the last mentioned would have resulted in the IRS Version! Eventually the name that seemed to be the most suitable was the New Revised Standard Version (NRSV).

Half-title pages are provided for each of the Testaments and for the Apocryphal/Deuterocanonical books of the Old Testament. The half-title page for the New Testament adopts the wording of the title page of the RSV New Testament when it first was published in 1946, namely, *The New Covenant, Commonly Called the New Testament of Our Lord and Savior Jesus Christ.* It occurred to me that it would be appropriate to devise a corresponding half-title page for the first part of the Bible. So I canvassed the members of the committee, soliciting their opinions on the suitability of adopting the following half-title page, *The Hebrew Scriptures, Commonly Called the Old Testament.* One member suggested *The Jewish Scriptures . . .* , but all the others approved the proposed wording. Editions of the Bible that include the Apocrypha have also the following half-title page, *The Apocryphal/Deuterocanonical Books of the Old Testament.*

The following list provides the name and affiliation of each member of the Standard Bible Committee as of May 19, 1989, when the Governing Board of the National Council of Churches, meeting at Louisville, Kentucky, adopted a resolution that "authorized and endorsed the New Revised Standard Version for use in worship, study and personal use, commending it to the churches for their use." An indication is added identifying whether the member served on the Old Testament or the New Testament panel.

William Beardslee, emeritus, Emory University (NT)

Phyllis A. Bird, Garrett-Evangelical Theological Seminary (OT)

George W. Coats, Lexington Theological Seminary (OT)

Demetrios J. Constantelos, Stockton State College, New Jersey (NT)

Robert C. Dentan, emeritus, General Theological Seminary (OT)

Alexander A. Di Lella, O.F.M., Catholic University of America (OT)

J. Cheryl Exum, Boston College (OT)

Reginald H. Fuller, emeritus, Protestant Episcopal Theological Seminary, Alexandria (NT)

Paul D. Hanson, Harvard Divinity School (OT)

Walter Harrelson, Vanderbilt Divinity School (OT)

William L. Holladay, Andover Newton Theological School (OT)

Sherman E. Johnson, emeritus, Church Divinity School of the Pacific (NT)

Robert A. Kraft, University of Pennsylvania (NT)

George M. Landes, Union Theological Seminary, N.Y. (OT)

Conrad E. L'Heureux, University of Dayton (OT)

S. Dean McBride, Jr., Union Theological Seminary, Richmond (OT)

Bruce M. Metzger, emeritus, Princeton Theological Seminary (NT)

Patrick D. Miller, Jr., Princeton Theological Seminary (OT)

Paul S. Minear, emeritus, Yale Divinity School (NT)

Lucetta Mowry, emerita, Wellesley College (NT)

Roland Murphy, O.Carm., emeritus, Duke Divinity School (OT)

Harry M. Orlinsky, Hebrew Union College/Jewish Institute of Religion (OT)

Marvin H. Pope, emeritus, Yale University (OT)

J. J. M. Roberts, Princeton Theological Seminary (OT)

Alfred von Rohr Sauer, emeritus, Christ Seminary Seminex, St. Louis (OT)

Katharine D. Sakenfeld, Princeton Theological Seminary (OT)

James A. Sanders, School of Theology at Claremont (OT)
Gene M. Tucker, Candler School of Theology, Emory University (OT)
Eugene C. Ulrich, University of Notre Dame (OT)
Allen Wikgren, emeritus, University of Chicago Divinity School (NT)

After Mr. and Mrs. Frederick W. Tripp, professional proofreaders of the Bible, and I had gone through three successive sets of galleys (with a combined weight of sixty-seven pounds of paper), the remaining task confronting me prior to the stage of transforming galleys into pages was to examine an alphabetical printout of all words and proper names in the Old Testament, Apocrypha, and New Testament in order to correct the computer's logic in hyphenating. By computer logic, for example, the word *antichrist* would have been hyphenated, had it come at the end of the line, as an-tich-rist! Other monstrosities, demanding correction, were ar-chan-gel, Co-elesyria, Da-thema, Leb-ba-eus, le-thech, and Re-cha-bites.

The work, which had involved a good many people, was at length finished, and on May 16, 1990, at the Episcopal Cathedral in Pittsburgh, the National Council of Churches held a service of blessing and commemoration of the New Revised Standard Version of the Bible. The sermon that I preached on that occasion was entitled "The Bible—Its Diversity and Its Unity."[2]

Seven publishers in the United States and in Great Britain were licensed to publish the New Revised Standard Version Bible, and within a few years the version was issued in more than seventy different sizes, formats, and bindings, and with a variety of maps, illustrations, and annotations. Denominations affiliated with the National Council of Churches adopted it for use in services of worship and in official publications.

As would be expected, following the publication of the NRSV I received a great variety of letters. Some expressed

---

[2]The sermon was chosen by James W. Cox for inclusion in *Best Sermons* 4 (San Francisco: HarperCollins, 1991).

approval and gratitude for the work of the committee, and others inquired why we had chosen to render this or that Hebrew or Greek word as we did. In answering such queries it was sometimes difficult to decide how deeply I should go into technical details. I usually responded that serious proposals for modification would be brought to the attention of the committee when, at a suitable time in the future, consideration would be given to all such matters.

Although the New Revised Standard Version had received the *imprimatur* from Roman Catholic authorities, it was felt desirable also to issue an edition with the Deutero-canonical books standing in their traditional places within the Old Testament. Professor Alexander Di Lella, a member of the Standard Bible Committee, was commissioned by the National Council of Churches to prepare such an edition for Roman Catholic readers. No changes were made in the wording of the translation, but the Catholic edition contains a special introduction prepared by Di Lella.

In Advent of 1993, several officials of the National Council of Churches, with Professor Di Lella and myself, were granted a private audience with Pope John Paul II in the Vatican. At that time a specially inscribed copy of the Catholic edition was presented to the pontiff, who expressed his appreciation that such an edition was now available.

As convener of the Standard Bible Committee, I have received a variety of invitations from colleges, seminaries, and congregations to speak about the committee's work in producing the new revision. Some of these invitations came to me directly; others were arranged through the department of publicity of the National Council of Churches. It was through the latter, for example, that I went to Los Angeles to be on the Tom Snyder program of WABC. On another occasion I participated in the Milt Rosenberg broadcast in the Chicago studios of WGN.

Each year in Great Britain, under the energetic direction of Gospatric Home, several hundred providers of church-related services and materials mount displays in

An audience with Pope John Paul II

booths at what is called the National Christian Resources Exhibition, usually held in the huge Exhibition Centre located at Sandown Park, Esher, in Surrey. I had been invited by Oxford Press to be present in May of 1991 at the seventh such exhibition, when the publishers of several English translations of the Scriptures mounted displays. The New International Version, produced in 1978, had a booth supervised by Dr. Kenneth L. Barker, who had been a member of the team of translators of that version. Oxford University Press displayed the newly published NRSV as well as the new British translation, the Revised English Bible (1989). With me to answer sundry questions raised by those who stopped at the Oxford booth was my long-time friend, Professor W. D. McHardy, the convener of the Revised English Bible Committee.

The acceptance in Britain of the NRSV Bible was gratifying. Within three years after it had become available, the Faculty of Divinity at Cambridge University voted to adopt

With two Bible translators, Kenneth L. Barker (NIV)
and W. D. McHardy (REB) in 1991

it as the recommended English version of the Bible for use
in undergraduate courses of religion at the university. Similar decisions were made at other British universities and
colleges.

In order to make the rendering of the NRSV still more
acceptable in Great Britain and Commonwealth nations, in
1994 Oxford University Press was granted permission to
produce an anglicized edition. This involved the introduction

of British spelling, grammar, and punctuation (single quotation marks instead of double), as well as the adoption of a limited number of changes in wording in order to replace Americanisms with expressions more usual to British readers. For the preparation of copy embodying such modifications, the Press secured the services of Roger Coleman, who had been in charge of the editorial administration and coordination of the work that resulted in the Revised English Bible.

In reviewing Coleman's work my task was focussed chiefly on evaluating the proposed alternatives that would replace Americanisms. Two considerations had to be balanced. On the one hand, it was desirable to limit the number of such changes, for the Anglicized edition was not intended to be a new translation. On the other hand, however, I was prepared to allow modifications—within the limits imposed by the Hebrew and Greek originals—of words and expressions that might appear to be odd or otherwise inappropriate to British readers.

By far the greatest number of such changes involved numerals. The American Committee had regularly omitted the word "and" in expressions such as "hundred fifty-three" (John 21:11), or "nine hundred sixty-nine" (Genesis 5:27), or "six hundred sixty-six" (Revelation 13:18), but Coleman urged that "and" be restored, and this I readily agreed to. I could also understand why "stump of Jesse" might well be altered to "stock of Jesse" (Isaiah 11:1); or "sated," to "glutted" (Lamentations 3:15); or "grainfields," to "cornfields" (Matthew 12:1); or "talk back," to "answer back" (Titus 2:9). But I could not see why "angels on horseback" needed to become "angels mounted on horses" (4 Maccabees 4:10) until I consulted *The Concise Oxford Dictionary of Current English* and learned that "angels-on-horseback" is a culinary expression meaning a "savoury of oysters wrapped in slices of bacon"!

Just prior to the publication of the Anglicized edition in the autumn of 1995, Oxford University Press arranged for me to spend ten days in Great Britain in order to make

Delivering a lecture at the First Midlands Christian Resources
Exhibition, Birmingham, October 1995

several presentations in London and elsewhere concerning
the development of the NRSV Bible. Besides invitations to
give an academic lecture on "Persistent Problems Confronting Bible Translators" at Cheltenham and Gloucester College, at Oak Hill Theological College, and at Selly Oak
Colleges, arrangements were also made for me to present a
popular lecture on "Handing Down the Bible through the

Ages—The Role of Scribe and Translator" at the First Midlands Christian Resources Exhibition at Birmingham, as well as a more theological lecture on "Eternal Word, Changing World: The Challenge and Promise of Biblical Translation" to the London Institute of Contemporary Christianity, an organization that had been launched several years earlier by Dr. John R. W. Stott.

The publication in 1952 of the Revised Standard Version of the Bible marked the beginning of the production of a great number of other translations of the Scriptures in English. From that year to the publication of the New Revised Standard Version in 1990, twenty-seven other English renderings of the complete Bible appeared, plus twenty-six additional renderings of the New Testament. These differ from one another to a greater or lesser degree depending in part on the translation theory that was followed[3] and in part on the level of readership for which each was prepared. During this period of nearly forty years, all these translators and revisers had devoted a simply staggering number of hours to patient, detailed scholarly work in trying to understand and express the meaning of the biblical writers' words and the organization of their ideas. Whatever advances have been made over the years in accuracy, clarity, and euphony of expression, such advances are the result of cooperation among and between scholars representing a broad spectrum of expertise and insight. One hopes that the slow accumulation of new insights arising from the research of many will result in renderings of Scripture that will continue to speak to the needs and understanding of successive generations of readers.

---

[3]The NRSV Committee followed the maxim, "As literal as possible, as free as necessary."

·∾· Chapter 9 ·∾·

THE SAGA OF THE YONAN CODEX

T HE afternoon of April 5, 1955, marked the opening of
an exhibition in the Great Hall of the Library of Congress that was to have extraordinary consequences.
Put on temporary display that day was a parchment manuscript of the Syriac New Testament called the Yonan Codex.
Its owner was a Washington-based businessman from Iran,
Mr. Norman Malek Yonan. Presiding at the ceremony,

The Yonan Codex, opened to Matthew 5:1ff. (the Beatitudes
begin at the middle of the last line on the right-hand page
and continue at the top of the left-hand page; see p. 115)

which opened with an invocation pronounced by the chaplain of the Senate, the Reverend Frederick Brown Harris, was the librarian of Congress, Dr. L. Quincy Mumford. Among the several governmental and ecclesiastical dignitaries who participated in the "unveiling" of the manuscript was the Honorable John Foster Dulles, secretary of state, who was the principal speaker[1] and who unveiled the booth where the codex was enclosed.

Two weeks earlier Yonan gained preliminary publicity for his manuscript when Washington newspapers announced that it had been insured for half an hour at an evaluation of one and a half million dollars during the time it was being taken by a procession of motorized police and armed guards from a bank vault of the National Savings and Trust Company of Washington to the White House. Here newspaper reporters and television cameras were focussed on President Eisenhower and Mr. Yonan bending over the manuscript, examining its pages. After leaving the White House the entourage went on to the Library of Congress, where the manuscript was temporarily deposited, awaiting the ceremony of opening its formal exhibition.

The next stage in the orchestration of publicity took place later that year when arrangements were made to take the manuscript, under armed guard, throughout the so-called Bible Belt of the South in order to exhibit it at various places and to solicit contributions in an attempt to raise three million dollars. Half of this amount was to be used to purchase the manuscript from Yonan in order to give it over permanently to the Library of Congress. The

---

[1] The remarks of Dulles (taken down stenographically) about "this wonderful old manuscript" were "informal and brief," as he stated, and were focussed chiefly on a verse from the Epistle to the Hebrews, "Wherefore seeing we also are compassed about with so great a cloud of witnesses . . . let us run with patience the race that is set before us" (12:1). A copy is on deposit among the Dulles papers in the Seeley Mudd Manuscript Library at Princeton University. For a photograph of Dulles opening the exhibition of the Yonan Codex, see *Bible Review* 12 (December 1996) 28.

other half was to be used to make facsimile copies of the codex available to institutions of higher learning; to publish a translation of its text in order to stimulate the study of the language of the manuscript; and "to promote other projects relevant to the dissemination of the faith and knowledge of Christianity."

The tour began on November 28, 1955, with what was doubtless an impressive ceremony at the Capitol plaza in Washington. There was newspaper, radio, and television coverage of the ceremony, which featured an address by Vice President Richard M. Nixon. Nixon declared, "This book of the Holy Scriptures will be taken to every city and hamlet in America in order that the American people may participate [i.e., by their contributions] in the ownership of this ancient manuscript."

A specially built glass-domed bus, equipped with a depository for the safe-keeping of the manuscript, was to take it under armed guard from place to place. Written on the sides of the bus, in large gold letters, was a sign that read, "Christendom's Most Precious Possession." Mrs. Cynthia Wadell, president of the National Council of Church Women, christened the bus, "The Spirit of Galilee," and expressed the belief that "all Americans will want to see it [the codex] and know its history." The well-known New York minister, the Reverend Dr. Norman Vincent Peale, wished for the tour Godspeed and success.

It was not surprising that such publicity attracted and impressed newspaper reporters, photographers, and radio and television crews. It was also not surprising that their accounts of the significance of the manuscript did not always correspond with the facts.

Before continuing with an account of the tour of "The Spirit of Galilee" and the subsequent fortunes of the Yonan Codex, it is necessary to provide a brief description of the manuscript and to relate how I became involved in the debate over the importance of the codex.

The Yonan Codex is a Syriac manuscript of the New Testament comprising 227 leaves of parchment, each measuring seven inches (27.5 cm) by eight and three-fourths inches (32.3 cm). The writing is in black ink, still quite legible, in single columns of twenty-nine or thirty lines per page. The text of the parchment folios begins with Matthew 9:35 and closes with Hebrews 12:9. Its present binding of boards includes at the beginning sixteen folios of paper of a much later date and four folios at the end, each page containing twenty-one or twenty-two lines of larger script; these provide in a totally different hand the portions of the text of Matthew and Hebrews lacking in the original parchment codex.

My examination of the Yonan Codex was made the previous year in response to an invitation from Mr. Yonan. It turned out that he had been trying to interest the Library of Congress in acquiring the manuscript, and Dr. Verner Clapp, assistant chief librarian of Congress, had suggested my name along with the names of several others[2] who would be qualified to give an estimate of the age and general importance of the document.

Having arrived at Washington, I was taken by Mr. Yonan to his lawyer's office where I waited until he brought from the vault a box containing the manuscript. He explained that it was a precious heirloom, for it had been in his family since about the fourth century. I examined the manuscript with care, comparing various passages with a copy of the Bible Society's printed Syriac New Testament that I had brought with me. In the passages that I collated, the text was identical with that of the standard Peshitta Syriac version. This version, made near the beginning of the fifth century, comprises twenty-two books of the New Testament (2 Peter, 2 and 3 John, Jude, and Revelation are absent).

In order to determine the approximate date of the manuscript I compared the style of its handwriting with

---

[2] I learned later that two other scholars from Princeton had also examined the manuscript, Philip K. Hitti, professor of Arabic at the University, and Henry S. Gehman, professor of Old Testament at the Seminary.

specimens of dated facsimiles in William H. P. Hatch's
Album of Dated Syriac Manuscripts[3] and came to the conclusion that the codex dated to about the seventh century at
the earliest, and was perhaps slightly later. After returning
home, I drafted a letter (dated July 2, 1954) to the librarian of
Congress in which, without mentioning any specific date or
monetary value of the manuscript, I recommended that the
library take steps to acquire it. As chair of the American
Committee on Versions of the International Greek New
Testament Project I was—and still am—interested in having
the Library of Congress increase its very modest collection
of biblical manuscripts.

A few months later an organization known as the
Aramaic Bible Foundation was incorporated with three
trustees: the Reverend William G. Adams, pastor of the
Temple Hills Baptist Church, Bethesda, Maryland; J. W.
Rixley Smith of Alexandria, Virginia, former assistant to
the late Senator Carter Glass; and Professor John Shapley, a
member of the art and archaeology department of the
Catholic University of America. With an office located in
Washington, D.C., the foundation produced a small brochure that was to be distributed during the tour of the
codex. The brochure began: "The Aramaic Bible Foundation presents the Yonan Codex, one of Christendom's most
precious documents, written in the language spoken by
Jesus and His disciples." More precisely, however, the language that Jesus spoke was Palestinian Aramaic, whereas
the language of the codex is Syriac, a related but somewhat
different Aramaic dialect.

In the light of this background information we may
now pick up the narrative of the subsequent fortunes of the
Yonan Codex during its progress through the Bible Belt.
The first stop made by the bus was at the chapel of the
Southern Baptist Theological Seminary in Louisville, Kentucky. Here Professor Shapley delivered a lecture on the
importance of the manuscript. Extravagant and misleading

---

[3]Boston: American Academy of Arts and Sciences, 1946.

claims were made as to its date and the nature of its text. According to information sent to me by W. D. Chamberlain, professor of New Testament at the Louisville Presbyterian Theological Seminary, Shapley claimed that the Yonan Codex was one of the oldest, if not the oldest manuscript of the New Testament. He also referred to it as a copy of the *original* New Testament in Aramaic.

After the lecture questions were invited, and Chamberlain began a series of inquiries that made it necessary for Shapley to admit that the codex was a copy of the Syriac Peshitta and that its text was, in fact, subsequent to the Old Syriac text.

That night Mr. Yonan flew to Louisville and the next morning he called at Chamberlain's office. He threatened Chamberlain with a lawsuit for defamation of character by having implied that Yonan was deliberately misleading the public. When Chamberlain showed that he was not easily intimidated, Yonan changed his tune and declared that just as Wycliffe and Tyndale were persecuted for bringing the Bible to the people, so too the clergy were still making things difficult for the Aramaic Bible Foundation in bringing the Yonan Codex to the attention of the public. He, of course, did not mention that a great difference was the attempt to raise three million dollars!

Chamberlain's letter to me included a most disquieting note. "I am writing you," he concluded, "because they are using your name as one who supports their claims and endorses them. I have seen a letter from you to the Librarian of Congress, dated July 2, 1954, which they are using. I do not see that you endorse what they claim. However, the letter itself is not publically shown but your name is used." Chamberlain added a final sentence: "I do not wish to involve you in any unpleasantness, but I did want you to know what was going on."

I had, in fact, previously learned from the librarian at Union Theological Seminary, Richmond, Virginia, that my name was being used in promotion designed to secure official sanction from the governor of Virginia and from the mayor of Richmond, in developing a campaign in the city and the state with the object of raising three million dollars for the Aramaic Bible Foundation. Consequently, on November 26, 1955, I had written to the Reverend William G. Adams, the president of the foundation, concluding my letter with the paragraph:

> I do not know the full details of the methods by which you are soliciting contributions in behalf of this Codex. I do not wish, however, to have my name used in the solicitation of funds, by mail or otherwise, because I should not wish to be charged with using the mails for purposes of defrauding, for which there are, you must know, very severe penalties.

Ten days later I received a curt response from Mr. Adams; it read as follows:

> Dear Dr. Metzger:
> This will acknowledge receipt of your recent letter. In the name of our Loving Lord—Whose we are and Whom we serve—I want to express my regret that you did not confer with us on a Christian basis.
> The contents of your letter have been noted, and in view of the statements and implications contained in your letter we have referred it to our counsel for such action as he may advise.
> In deference to your wishes, we shall not use your name in connection with the accomplishment of the objectives of the Aramaic Bible Foundation, which has received the plaudits, approval, and encouragement of many national leaders in the political, religious, theological and scholastic fields.

Another angle to the affair emerged when J. Philip Hyatt, professor of Old Testament at the School of Religion at Vanderbilt University, Nashville, Tennessee, wrote me on December 10, 1955:

> Dear Metzger:
> I have just had a conference with two men, one of whom introduced himself as a Rev. Mr. Adams, a Baptist minister from Washington, D.C., and the other a Mr. Hendrickson.

They have talked with me about the Yonan (spelling?) manuscript, and seemed a bit surprised when I did not agree with their enthusiasm for it. They are apparently promoting an appearance of it in Nashville early in January, at which time it will be "blessed" (or something of the sort!) by the governor of Tennessee, etc. etc.

I understand that you have actually seen this manuscript, and have an opinion as to its commercial value—which is considerably less than the owners are trying to get out of the government for it. I am writing to you with two purposes in mind: (1) would you write and tell me briefly your opinion of the MS. and its value (vis à vis other Syriac MSS. of course); and (2) if, as it appears, an attempt is being made to build up this MS. to some very high figure, is there anything that SBL [The Society of Biblical Literature], or some group from SBL (such as the Textual Criticism Seminar), might do to give the public a true picture of the nature of this MS? I am vice-president of SBL now, and slated (I assume) to be elected president later this month. The publicity I have seen appears to be attempting to make people believe this is the oldest Biblical MS. in existence, in the original language spoken by Jesus. Of course it is no such thing; even Mr. Adams did not claim that, but did not seem to care that Syriac, as a form of eastern Aramaic, is not the same as the Western Aramaic of Palestine.

A brief note from you would be appreciated, and I look forward at least to seeing you at the SBL meetings in New York.

Acting on Hyatt's suggestion, I drafted a proposed memorandum about the Yonan Codex, and at the annual meeting of the Society of Biblical Literature, held later that month in New York at Union Theological Seminary, I showed copies of it to Professor William H. P. Hatch and Professor William F. Albright. The latter, who made one or two suggested changes in the wording, agreed to join Hatch and me in presenting the memorandum to the society. That night I returned to Princeton to type the final copy and to make several hundred mimeographed copies for distribution at the business meeting of the society the next day. At that time, without much discussion, the society adopted the following statement, with no negative vote being cast.

> The Society of Biblical Literature at its annual meeting in New York City on December 28–30, 1955, wishes to go on record as opposing some of the publicity attending the efforts currently being made to raise by popular subscription $1,500,000 for the purchase of the so-called Yonan Codex. This codex is a manuscript of the Syriac New Testament which is reported to be "the oldest surviving complete New Testament written in Syriac-Aramaic, the language spoken by Jesus" (Washington *Evening Star,* March 25, 1955).

> According to members of our Society who have examined the manuscript, the Yonan Codex is a copy of the Syriac Peshitta, a version which was made from the Greek New Testament at about the beginning of the fifth century and which contains twenty-two of the twenty-seven books of the New Testament. Edessene Syriac, the language of this version, differs considerably[4] from the Palestine Aramaic used by Jesus more than four centuries earlier. About three hundred manuscripts of the Peshitta version are known to exist in the libraries of this country and Europe. Several of these are older than the Yonan Codex, which some of our members who are expert in Syriac palaeography date to the seventh or eighth century. According to certain members of the Society who have frequently arranged for the purchase of biblical manuscripts, a fair estimate of the value of a manuscript like the Yonan Codex is about $5,000.

Now the fat was in the fire. It was not surprising that the media picked up the story and ran with it. Hyatt, as the newly elected president of the society, and other members were interviewed by the press, and the Aramaic Bible Foundation issued "clarifying" statements. The following week the lawyer of the foundation wrote to Hyatt, threatening a lawsuit against the society for libel if it did not retract the statement voted at the business session.

---

[4]My initial draft had the word "somewhat"; at Albright's suggestion this was changed to "considerably."

Meanwhile, I prepared an article for the *Christian Century* magazine entitled "Is the Yonan Codex Unique?" Two lawyers (my father and the magazine's lawyer) reviewed what I had written; after several changes were made in the wording, it was published in the issue of February 22, 1956. Here, among other points, I tried to put the Yonan manuscript in the context of other similar copies of the Peshitta Syriac version. I pointed out that, far from being unique, several hundred other manuscript copies of the Peshitta New Testament have been catalogued in libraries and museums of the United States and Europe, and some of them are earlier in date than the Yonan copy.

After further negotiations with the foundation's lawyer, and with understandable anxiety lest a lawsuit deplete the society's modest financial resources, Hyatt consulted the other officers of the society and the twenty associates-in-council, as they were called (the function of the latter group was roughly similar to that of trustees of the society). Sixteen of the twenty despaired of being successful in a court of law defending the society's action, fearing that neither the court nor the public would understand the technical linguistic arguments. Consequently, as the least unsatisfactory resolution of the affair, it was decided that Hyatt should send the following letter, dated March 5, 1956, to the Aramaic Bible Foundation.

Dear Sirs:

The Council of the Society of Biblical Literature and Exegesis regret the misunderstanding which has arisen between the Society and the Aramaic Bible Foundation. The resolution which was adopted by the Society on December 29, 1955, was not intended to discredit the Aramaic Bible Foundation or the owner of the Yonan Codex. The resolution did not intend to give the impression that Syriac, the language of the Codex, was an entirely different language from that spoken by Jesus. Qualified scholars know that Syriac is an Aramaic dialect and is related to that dialect of Aramaic spoken by Jesus. The monetary appraisal of the Codex expressed the opinion of some members of the Society; the great majority of members are not in position to make such an appraisal. As to the date of the Codex we recognize the possibility of honest difference of scholarly opinion; we have been informed that at least two qualified scholars, who are members of the Society, had subscribed to a fifth-century date.

We have been informed by Mr. Norman Yonan and the Aramaic Bible Foundation that it is not the intention of Mr. Yonan to profit from the transfer of the Codex to the Foundation, which will in turn place it in the Library of Congress. The Foundation further informs us that the funds which it is seeking to raise will, after the payment of the necessary expenses, be devoted to the establishment of professorships for the teaching of Aramaic in theological seminaries, the offering of scholarships especially for the study of Aramaic, and the publishing of facsimiles, translations and studies of the Yonan Codex. Such a program is consistent with the interests of the Society of Biblical Literature and Exegesis, and we hope that these objectives will be accomplished.

> Yours truly,
> J. Philip Hyatt
> President (1956)

In a later communication to me Hyatt commented, "There seems to be no 'right' way to deal with these people [i.e., the Aramaic Bible Foundation]. I would make no claim that our way was entirely right. I do hope that some people who see our latest statement will take the trouble to read it carefully, and thus see what it actually says and what it does not say. . . . I interpret it as a clarification of our position and a gesture of conciliation. Our resolution still stands, and individual opinions are not silenced." Ironically enough, while the clarification removed the threat of a lawsuit against the society, in its continuing publicity the foundation used the statement as the society's approval of the extravagant claims being made for the Yonan Codex!

Subsequent fortunes of the Yonan Codex can be more briefly recounted. After it had been displayed at a political function involving Governor A. B. ("Happy") Chandler of Kentucky, the entourage went on to Little Rock, Arkansas, and from there to Dallas, Texas. Here the manuscript was placed, under suitable armed guard, on display in the Nieman Marcus Department Store. Shortly thereafter the Dallas representative of the American Bible Society got in touch with the society's headquarters in New York for suggestions on how to respond to a barrage of queries that the exhibition had generated. I have no doubt that Dr. Eric M. North, general secretary of the Bible Society, would have responded in much the same vein as he did in his letter to me of January 4, 1956, when he wrote:

> May I express my satisfaction at your efforts in the Society of Biblical Literature to put an end to the extravagant claims about the so-called Yonan Codex.

> There are a lot of people trying to trade on religion in a dishonest manner and I am glad to see some of them caught up with.

During the following months the tour of the glass-domed bus with its "treasure" came to an end. How much money had been collected was not revealed.

A few years later the manuscript surfaced once again, this time in Georgia. In a letter dated May 31, 1960, Edwin D. Johnston, professor of Bible at Mercer University in Macon, Georgia, informed me that the Yonan Codex had been given to the university by Mr. Yonan, then a resident of Lawrenceville, Georgia. Dr. Harry Smith, a Mercer alumnus and executive secretary of the Baptist Foundation, had been, Johnston said, "greatly responsible for interesting Mr. Yonan in giving the Codex to Mercer."

Johnston's letter requested that I send him suggestions concerning the proper way of preserving and protecting such manuscripts. He also requested my judgment on the advisability of having the manuscript microfilmed. Of course, I recommended that it be microfilmed and that a copy be sent to the archives of the International Greek New Testament Project at Claremont, California.

More than a decade later, during the summer of 1973, having decided to make inquiry of the librarian at Mercer concerning the Yonan Codex, I received the following reply from Daniel Lamar Metts, Jr.

> The manuscript was given to us in May 1960 and was returned to Mr. Yonan in 1962. This happened before I came here. Apparently there was continuing disagreement between Mr. Yonan and the University concerning copying the manuscript for study or publication and financial benefits from copies. I am not clear on details. I have no idea at all what happened to the document since. I am sorry not to be of more help, but that is all I know.

Curiously enough, several year later while I was attending sessions of the annual meeting of the American Academy of Religion, Dr. Paul L. Garber, professor of Bible at Agnes Scott College, Decatur, Georgia, casually inquired of me whether I had ever heard of the Yonan Codex. This led to a most astonishing disclosure. The manuscript, Garber told me, was in the possession of the Emotional Maturity Instruction Center, Decatur, Georgia.[5] The center had transliterated the Syriac text of the Beatitudes in Christ's Sermon on the Mount (Matthew 5:3–12) and was making a copy of this available for four dollars with the assurance that, by concentrating each day on these sentences in Aramaic, one's personality would become adjusted and more mature. In fact, according to Garber the center had even persuaded magistrates in Atlanta to buy copies of the transliteration for use in attempting to quell obstreperous prisoners!

For several years thereafter I heard nothing more concerning the Yonan Codex. Then in the autumn of 1994,

---

[5]In response to my writing for further information the center sent several typescript booklets: "Rationale and Guidelines for Emotional Maturity Instruction," three levels of "Keys to Human Relations," and "A Promising New Approach to Rehabilitation," the last by Dr. C. D. Warren, former medical director, Georgia Department of Corrections. These, as well as copies of several testimonial letters, are now on deposit in the archives of Princeton Theological Seminary library.

it surfaced once again, this time in Michigan. During a visit to Western Theological Seminary in Holland, Michigan, where I had been invited to give several lectures, I was taken to visit a newly established museum containing early printed Bibles and other treasures near Grand Haven, bordering on Lake Michigan. This museum, established by Mr. Robert Van Kampen, is named The Scriptorium: Center for Christian Antiquities. During my visit the director, Dr. Scott T. Carroll, showed me some of the center's treasures, including several manuscripts in Greek, Latin, Coptic, and Hebrew. Then he took from a shelf a parchment codex about seven by nine inches. When he identified it as the Yonan Codex, one can imagine my surprise—not to say amazement.

Of course I asked how it had come into the possession of the Scriptorium, and learned that it had been acquired for about $25,000 at an auction at Sotheby's. Holding now in my hands the same manuscript that I had examined forty years earlier released a flood of memories. I realized that at last the saga of "The Yonan Codex Affair" had come to a conclusion; the manuscript was now ensconced in a suitable environment and available for scholarly examination and research. Certainly the ancient comment made by Terentianus Maurus is altogether applicable:

Habent sua fata libelli.
(Books have their fates.)

Chapter 10

CONDENSING THE BIBLE

D URING the mid-1970s the editors of the Reader's Digest Condensed Books projects gave long and serious consideration to the question of whether to issue a condensation of the Bible. On the one hand, they had published many classics in condensed form that appealed to a wide spectrum of readers—and certainly the Bible qualifies as a classic. On the other hand, they naturally did not wish to alienate some of their clientele who might consider it sacrilegious to condense the Bible.

After becoming convinced that such a project would, on the whole, be welcomed, the Reader's Digest editors made inquiries among various persons as to which English version of the Bible should be chosen as the text to be condensed. When I received such an inquiry I replied that for several reasons the Revised Standard Version of 1952 appeared to me to be the most suitable for condensation: it was in wide use, its scholarship was generally acknowledged, it enjoyed an established familiarity, and it was linked to the King James Version, thus preserving echoes of the elevated and dignified tone cherished by so many generations of Bible readers.

Some months later I received a letter from Herbert H. Lieberman, executive editor of Condensed Books Projects, inviting me to serve as general editor of *The Reader's Digest Bible*, to be condensed from the Revised Standard Version. My responsibilities, he said, would be to advise which block cuts could be made in each biblical book. After the final editing had been accomplished by Reader's Digest editors, I was to review their work and to discuss with Lieberman all points still at issue.

In March of 1978, the vice president of Reader's Digest, John T. Beaudouin, arranged for an initial meeting of the members of the team who were to be involved in the project. This meeting, which lasted for two days, was held at the Holiday Inn of Mount Kisco, located not far from Pleasantville, New York, the headquarters of Reader's Digest. After mutual introductions had been made, Beaudouin laid out plans for the project. Unlike other "shorter Bibles," this edition would not omit any of the sixty-six books. The aim was to produce a text, shortened and clarified, yet preserving every incident, personality, and teaching of substance, while keeping the essence and flavor of the familiar language of Scripture. It was not meant to be an "easy" version that eliminated harsh or difficult passages.

Following this preliminary meeting, I set to work listing those passages that might well be eliminated because the same account is repeated elsewhere. For example, Psalm 14 and Psalm 53 are virtually identical in wording. The seventh chapter of Numbers repeats twelve times an identical enumeration of the components of the daily offering made by the representative of each of the twelve tribes of Israel. Furthermore, I considered such passages as the genealogies in Genesis, 1 Chronicles, Ezra, and Nehemiah, as well as many of the dietary laws in Leviticus, to be expendable in a condensed edition of the Scriptures.

On the other hand, occasionally it seemed wise to retain an account of the same incident in more than one book when the structure of the narrative seemed to require it. For example, the temptation of Jesus is still recounted in each of the three Synoptic Gospels, and the miracle of the multiplication of loaves and fishes to feed five thousand people remains in all four Gospels.

Secondly, I drew up a list of other passages that were not to be modified in any way, not even by the elimination of a single word. This list included the Ten Commandments, Psalm 23, the Beatitudes in Matthew 5, the Lord's Prayer, John 3:16, chapter 13 of 1 Corinthians, and others. Likewise, I searched through earlier series of the International Sunday School Lessons for verses that had frequently been identified as "Golden Texts." These too were to remain without alteration.

Thirdly, I insisted that when a transitional sentence was formed in order to link together two sections remaining after a block had been excised, no word or expression was to be used that did not belong to the vocabulary of the Revised Standard Version.

After my proposals of passages that could be eliminated had been approved, John E. Walsh (the editor with whom I had the most frequent contact) and his team used, so to speak, the scalpel, and, with expertise gained over many years, carefully excised a few words here and there throughout the text. For example, the four words in the expression, "he answered and said," were usually reduced by 50 percent to "he answered." In John 4:14 the second instance of the phrase, "the water that I shall give him," was replaced by "it."

At the conclusion of this kind of detailed work of condensation, a typescript of each book of the Bible was submitted to me for examination and approval. Sometimes I would make further suggestions, either by way of restoring deleted material or occasionally by making additional deletions. In most instances of disagreement, the office at Pleasantville deferred to my opinion.

At the end of four years of such cooperative work, the condensed version of the biblical text had been reduced by about 40 percent. The Old Testament, with its greater variety in form and content, offered larger scope than the New Testament for reduction. It was shortened by approximately one half, different books permitting different percentages of reduction. The New Testament, much sparer in form and language, was brought down by about one quarter.

My assignment also involved the preparation of brief, nontechnical introductions to the Old and the New

Testaments and to each individual book. Limited to using no more than about three hundred words for each book, I found it exceedingly difficult to say concisely what needed to be conveyed concerning the author, date, literary style, and any special features of a given book. Whenever feasible, I tried also to show the influence of an Old Testament book upon the New Testament. Most of these brief introductions were rewritten several times.

Since the condensed version of the Bible was not intended to be a study edition, coordinated with reference books and concordances, but rather a reading Bible, it was decided that neither chapter nor verse numbers would be necessary. In this respect the edition resembles the early manuscripts of the Hebrew and Greek originals, which, of course, had no chapter and verse divisions. The chapter numbers that are found in most English Bibles date from the twelfth century and are the work of Stephen Langton, who later became archbishop of Canterbury. The verse numbers in English Bibles are of still more recent origin; they appear first in the Geneva Bible of 1560.

In order to assist the reader in locating passages in the condensation, the editors at Pleasantville drew up an extensive index of persons, places, incidents, and teachings in the Bible. Since these are keyed to the text by page, a reader who may not know where to find, for example, the book of Judges for the account of Samson and Delilah is able to locate the passage at once by consulting the index.

As would be expected, following the publication of *The Reader's Digest Bible* in September of 1982 I began to receive many letters, pro and con. The number of those who wrote objecting to its production outnumbered those who told me they liked it. Not a few inquired whether I had never read Revelation 22:18–19, where woe is pronounced against those who "add to or take away from the words of the book of this prophecy."

I would usually reply that the condensed version was not at all intended to do away with the complete Bible; it was intended for those who were daunted by the length of the entire Bible, thinking it too long and formidable even to begin reading it. By starting with a condensation, such persons might be stimulated to read the complete Bible. Furthermore, the warning in the book of Revelation against adding to or taking away words really amounts to something like a copyright notice. Such warnings were not unusual when manuscripts were copied by hand and the basic text could easily be altered. Eusebius, the early church historian, tells us that Bishop Irenaeus of Lyons in Gaul placed a similar warning at the close of his treatise *On the Ogdoad,* which he considered especially liable to suffer intentional corruption by scribes. In such cases the warning means that scribes should beware of adding material or dropping material from the copy that was being made, and then claiming that it was a true and faithful copy.

Among the many letters that I received, two may be mentioned in particular. One of them, an anonymous letter postmarked Brooklyn, New York, began:

> This is from a Christian who is so cut up over what you and your so-called friends have done by rewriting the Bible. It would give me great pleasure if I had a bus or a jeep and could run you down, and then prop you up and run you down again. May you and your family be cast into the pit of hell. You bitch of all bitches, who gave you the write [*sic*] to do this? You shall die early for what you did.

After much more in a similar vein on both sides of a long sheet of ruled paper, the writer concluded with the statement, "I am enclosing some curse powder that I trust will have its proper effect." When I opened the envelope something like unscented talcum power sifted out, but having read the letter I had no inclination to investigate the nature of the powder! I merely put the letter in my file marked "crack-pot letters."

The other letter, written by a woman who said she was living in a retirement home near Philadelphia and had for years subscribed to the Reader's Digest Condensed Books, was altogether different. It began:

When I heard that the Reader's Digest was putting out a condensation of the Bible, I was shocked, having read Rev. 22:18. So I did not order the book. However, through an error I received the Bible and intended to return the package unopened. On second thought, and knowing that I had a week to look it over before returning it, I opened the package—and I LIKE IT. . . . I have read Hebrews and Romans, two books hard for me. I will keep my R. D. Bible and use it. Again many thanks.

(signed)

It was several letters like the second that compensated for the labor I had expended in producing the condensed edition.

In the autumn of 1982 a letter arrived from a certain Mr. Roy McConnell, the producer of the Canadian television program called "Front Page Challenge," inviting me to come to Toronto in order to participate in the program for December 19th. Then in its twenty-sixth year of consecutive weekly broadcasts, the format of a typical program involved the rapid and vigorous interrogation by a team of four panelists in order to discover the identity and occupation of the guest "challenger"—whom the members of the panel could hear but not see. Over the previous quarter of a century a wide variety of guests had been quizzed, including Art Buchwald, Jack Dempsey, Zsa Zsa Gabor, Dorothy Kilgallen, Ralph Nader, Rosa Parks, Mary Pickford, Eleanor Roosevelt, Morley Safer, Benjamin Spock, and many others—but no biblical scholars![1]

Among the members of the panel whom I recall most vividly was Gordon Sinclair, then in his eighty-second year.

---

[1] In 1981 the Canadian Broadcasting Company published a volume surveying the development of the program over the preceding quarter of a century, with a list of the names of hundreds of guests (*Front Page Challenge: The 25th Anniversary,* by Alex Barris). After thirty-eight years of broadcasting, the program came to an end in April of 1995.

According to Pat Pearce, the television critic for the *Montreal Star,* "Front Page Challenge gets good guests and has a fine, professional gloss. But it's the perpetual Peck's bad boy, Sinclair, who gives it consistent—if occasionally irritating—vitality." George Lonn's book *Faces of Canada* listed—presumably as a public service—a string of epithets that had been aimed at Gordon Sinclair: "Cocky . . . loudmouthed . . . conceited . . . atheistic . . . brash . . . touchy . . . temperamental . . . self-made . . . rich . . . low-brow . . . nationalistic." Someone in the studio prior to the interview alerted me that probably Sinclair would ask about financial arrangements and how much I had been paid. In due course this question was put, and I responded that I was paid a flat sum for what I did and received no royalties.

At the end of about fifteen minutes of questioning no one on the panel had been successful in probing my identity or the reason why I had been selected to appear on the program, and so the panel turned its attention to the second challenger that evening. This was a government administrator from Yellowknife, capital of the Northwest Territories. In this instance, the panel was successful in identifying the person and his position.

During the following months and years other editions and translations of the condensed Bible were produced. A three-volume edition printed with large type (totalling 2,983 pages) and a separate index volume of 125 pages were published. In September of 1983 a British edition entitled *The Reader's Bible* was issued in London; it contained a foreword written by Dr. Donald Coggan, former archbishop of Canterbury. Mr. David Blomfield of the Reader's Digest Association, Ltd., arranged for my wife and me to be present at the launching of the volume. We were housed in a suite at Hotel Chesterfield on Charles Street, Mayfair, and, with the Coggans, were entertained at a pleasant dinner party. Following a conference at the London Press Centre, I made an appearance on one of the British television channels for an interview concerning the process of condensing the Bible.

The popularity of the condensed Bible in English led to the publication of similar editions in other languages. In 1985 an Italian edition was issued (with the *imprimatur*), entitled *La Bibbia: Edizione condensata di selezione dal Reader's Digest.* Since it contained also the Deuterocanonical books and was adorned with a good many pictures, some in color, the volume was considerably larger and heavier than the English version. Following in general the grid used for the original condensation, the work was overseen by two academics, Professor Gianfranco Ravasi and Professor Giovanni Saldarini. For the scriptural base they made use of the Italian translation, *La Sacra Bibbia,* published in 1971 by the Conferenza Episcopale Italiana. Besides presenting a copy to Pope John Paul II, Ravasi and Saldarini were interviewed on two television channels. According to information sent to Lieberman at the Pleasantville office, "the press in general had a positive reaction, apart from the newspaper *L'unità* (which is the organ of the Communist Party!)." In 1990 a French illustrated edition was published in Paris and a British illustrated edition was published in London.

The project of preparing a Korean version of the condensed Bible was less happy. In order to accomplish its production in the least amount of time, nine different translators worked simultaneously on various parts of the volume. As might have been anticipated, their combined work was far from homogeneous, particularly since, as it turned out, one or two of the translators had not been accustomed to reading the Bible and were therefore not acquainted with its style and vocabulary. Consequently, what was intended to be a speedy process became quite lengthy, since much of the work needed to be redone. The volume was finally published in 1987.

In looking back over the years that I devoted to the preparation of the condensed Bible, I have only the most pleasant recollections of my personal contacts with all who participated in this cooperative venture.

Chapter II

LITERARY FORGERIES

ONE of the more interesting courses that I took during my graduate work in classics at Princeton University was Duane Reed Stuart's seminar on Latin epigraphy. This course opened my eyes to the immense number of inscribed stones and metals preserved from antiquity in various degrees of mutilation. Taken together they provide the modern scholar with a considerable amount of information for the reconstruction of the political, social, military, economic, and religious history of the ancient Roman world.

Among the tens of thousands of entries of Latin inscriptions cited in the fifteen huge volumes of the *Corpus Inscriptionum Latinarum,* here and there the identifying number assigned to an inscription is followed by an asterisk. Instead of calling attention, as one might suppose, to a particularly important inscription, the asterisk designates an epigraphical forgery.

It was disconcerting to learn that the proportion of spurious or suspected Latin inscriptions to authentic inscriptions is about one to thirteen. The most prolific forger during the late Renaissance period seems to have been Pirro Ligorio, the successor to Michelangelo in supervising the work at St. Peter's in Rome; he was responsible for 2,995 of the 3,645 spurious inscriptions in *CIL,* volume VI, part 5! Ligorio's audacity was incredible. Many of his forgeries he pretended to have found in gardens and libraries of well-known houses in Rome, and as a rule he mentioned the exact location. He carried his work even to the point of carving more than a hundred of his forgeries in stone, many of them for his patron, the cardinal of Carpi. The true character of most of the forgeries was not discovered until long after they had been perpetuated; in the meantime they were copied into new collections by scholars all over the world.

My studies took me into the discipline of palaeography, and I became acquainted with the fraudulent activities in the nineteenth century of a Greek named Constantine Simonides. Observing that museums and collectors of ancient documents were willing to pay high prices for ancient manuscripts, this enterprising palaeographer began to provide quantities of Greek texts professing to be of fabulous antiquity. These included a copy of Homer in an almost prehistoric style of writing, a copy of the Gospel according to Matthew, written fifteen years after the Ascension (!), and other parts of the New Testament—such as portions of the Epistles of James and of Jude from the first century. These productions enjoyed a short period of notoriety and were then exposed as forgeries.

Among the scholars who helped to expose Simonides was Constantin Tischendorf, the discoverer of Codex Sinaiticus. In retaliation, and while staunchly maintaining the genuineness of his other productions, Simonides admitted that he had written *one* manuscript that passed as being very ancient—and that was Codex Sinaiticus! Simonides's scheme of taking revenge was ingenious, but it did not stand up to investigation. Apart from internal evidence of the script itself, it was shown that Simonides could not have accomplished his copying prior to the time that Tischendorf first acquired some leaves of the codex in 1844.

Over the years, further reading brought to my attention wide-ranging accounts of frauds perpetrated by English, German, Irish, Italian, and Scottish forgers. One of the more sophisticated was Thomas J. Wise, an honorary fellow of Worcester College, Oxford. Bibliographer, collector, and editor, Wise assembled the great Ashley Library, later acquired by the British Museum. His reputation was damaged when in 1934 it was proved that a large number of rare pamphlets purporting to be first editions of writings of Victorian authors, copies of which were in the Ashley Library, were in fact forgeries. The authors include the Brownings, George Eliot, Kipling, Ruskin, Swinburne, Tennyson, and Thackeray.

My interest in the subject of literary frauds and pseudepigrapha eventually led to my decision to discuss the subject, "Literary Forgeries and Canonical Pseudepigrapha," as my presidential address in 1971 at the annual meeting of the Society of Biblical Literature.[1] In drawing up an extensive bibliography on the subject, I came upon J. A. Farrer's classic book *Literary Forgeries,* which was also translated into German. In the opening paragraph of a chapter entitled "Forgery in the Church," Farrer writes:

> Forgery, which has invaded every department of literary activity, has made its most complete conquests and left its most indelible marks in the field of ecclesiastical literature. The composition of works in support of definite ends, though it long preceded the Christian era, seems to have acquired increased impetus after the introduction of the new religion had supplied new motives for fictitious writing.[2]

The list begins with the correspondence between Christ and King Abgar of Edessa and that between Seneca and Paul. And as centuries continued, these fictions increased in volume, until at last we reach that gigantic hagiological work known as *Acta Sanctorum,* collected by the Bollandists in sixty-four huge volumes which began to be published in Antwerp in 1643 and which it took many generations of Jesuit scholars 240 years to complete. It is, Farrer comments, "perhaps the most astonishing literary enterprise that the world can show, though certainly as historically worthless as it is wonderful in execution."

Not mentioned by Farrer are the animated controversies that were aroused in the eighteenth century when a

[1] *Journal of Biblical Literature* 91 (1972) 3–24.
[2] London: Longmans, Green, & Co., 1907, 126.

German scholar, Christoph M. Pfaff, announced that he had discovered three Greek fragments of Irenaeus, which he promptly published. But he could never show the manuscript in which he had discovered them or direct anyone to it in any library. Some scholars denied that the fragments were all from the pen of Irenaeus, but no one ventured to suggest that they might have been forged by a man of such reputation and scholarly attainment as Pfaff, professor of theology and chancellor at the University of Tübingen, the discoverer and editor of many patristic manuscripts. It was not until 1900 that the Irenaeus fragments were shown by Harnack to be a fabrication of Pfaff, and no one takes the material seriously today. Incidents like this make it plain that if learning is to make sound progress in the discovery of ancient texts, every precaution must be taken to verify such claims.

In addition to my reading about literary forgeries produced in previous centuries, it has been my lot to be acquainted with several persons who either may have perpetrated a literary fabrication or were the victim of such a hoax.

An Alleged Fragment of Clement of Alexandria

In 1958 Morton Smith, an erudite professor of ancient history at Columbia University, was preparing a catalogue of the books in the library of the Greek Orthodox monastery of Mar Saba, southeast of Jerusalem in the Judean desert. One day he came upon a seventeenth-century printed book that contained the Greek text of part of a letter, written on the last two (unprinted) pages of the book and running over for a half-page onto the binder's paper at the back; here it breaks off abruptly. The heading of the letter states that it had been taken from a collection of letters of Clement of Alexandria.

The content of the letter is sufficiently tantalizing, for it discloses that Clement claims to be acquainted with three forms of the Gospel according to Mark: one is in the New Testament; another is a Carpocratian gnostic gospel called to Clement's attention by Theodore, the unknown person to whom he is writing; and the third is a gospel preserved in the church of Alexandria, which (according to Clement) is kept guarded and is read only to initiates. This "secret gospel" contains some, but not all, of the extra material put forward by the Carpocratians.

During the months following his return to the United States, Smith circulated copies of his transcription of the Greek text of Clement's letter to a number of his colleagues, from whom he invited comments. I could never make up my mind whether the text was a forgery—ancient or modern. Several palaeographers to whom Smith had made photographs of the text available dated the handwriting between the late seventeenth and the early nineteenth century. It is striking that the text contains none of the errors typical in manuscript transmission (see the comment by Murgia in n. 10 on p. 131 below).

After a long period of gestation, in 1973 Smith published two books devoted to his find: a scholarly publication entitled *Clement of Alexandria and a Secret Gospel of Mark* and a popular book entitled *The Secret Gospel: The Discovery and Interpretation of the Secret Gospel according to Mark.*[3]

The gist of Smith's interpretation is that the "secret gospel" was an independent, relatively primitive source prior to the canonization of Mark and the other three Gospels. Taking Clement's two quotations from the secret gospel as a credible reflection of the actual conduct of Jesus, Smith developed the theory that Jesus was a magician who practiced a secret nocturnal initiation of individual disciples, involving baptism and an ecstatic experience of ascent into the heavens—the whole thing with homosexual overtones. This, according to Smith, was what was "going on" at Gethsemane when Jesus was arrested.

The whole account does credit to Smith's ability to enter into the spirit of the Carpocratians, who did indeed

---

[3]Cambridge: Harvard University Press, 1973; New York: Harper & Row, 1973.

make use of the Christian gospels in order to convey an impression of libertinism of this kind. Smith's determination to see the secret gospel as primitive, and as telling him something he wished to know about Jesus, is extraordinary. More than once he indulges in conjectural emendation of the text of the secret gospel or the canonical Gospels in order to neutralize or to remove something that would interfere with his reconstruction.

Ten years following the publication of the "secret gospel" Smith issued in the *Harvard Theological Review*[4] a rather self-serving "tally" of how his project was being received. "The Score at the End of the First Decade," as the subtitle of the article phrases it, showed general but not universal support for Smith's interpretations. Those who thought that the letter was not by Clement included A. D. Nock, Munck, Völker, Kümmel, Murgia, Musurillo, and Quesnell.

The most serious challenge to Smith was Quentin Quesnell's series of queries in the *Catholic Biblical Quarterly*[5] that concluded with the simple colloquy: "Is there a reasonable possibility of forgery? The answer, working only with the evidence that Smith presents, seems to be clearly, yes."

Although Quesnell never said directly that he thought it was Smith who had forged the Clement fragment, Jacob Neusner, a former student of Smith's and editor of an earlier Festschrift honoring Smith, has had no such reluctance. Writing in the *Bulletin for Biblical Research,* Neusner declared:

> In what must now be declared the forgery of the century, the very integrity of the quest for the historical Jesus was breached . . . by Morton Smith, whose "historical" results— Jesus was "really" a homosexual magician—depended upon

---

[4]"Clement of Alexandria and Secret Mark: The Score at the End of the First Decade," 75 (1982) 449–61.

[5]"The Mar Saba Clementine: A Question of Evidence," 37 (1975) 48–67.

a selective believing in whatever Smith thought was historical. Even at the time, some of us told Smith to his face that
he was an upside down fundamentalist, believing anything
bad anybody said about Jesus, but nothing good.[6]

Less emotional and more probative is Ernest Best's
careful analysis showing that the two quotations from secret
Mark contain substantially more "Markan" stylistic traits
than does a passage of similar length from the canonical
Mark.[7] Best concludes that the secret gospel "is too much
like Mark, and therefore should be regarded as a deliberate
imitation of Mark's style."

A few years later Eric Osborn published a comprehensive review of recent research on Clement,[8] in which he
concludes that the letter is a pious forgery by someone who
successfully imitated Clement's style but misunderstood
Clement's idea concerning secret tradition.

Still more recently, A. H. Criddle, making use of
statistical analysis, has argued that "the letter proper (i.e.,
excluding the heading and the extracts from the secret
gospel), contains too high a ratio of Clementine to non-
Clementine traits to be authentic and should be regarded as
a deliberate imitation of Clement's style"[9]

This is not the place to debate further the authenticity
of the secret gospel.[10] It is enough to point out the absence

---

[6]Jacob Neusner, "Who Needs 'The Historical Jesus'? An
Essay-Review," *Bulletin for Biblical Research* 4 (1994) 116.

[7]At the close of his review of E. J. Pryke's *Redactional Style in
the Marcan Gospel* (*Journal for the Study of the New Testament* 4 [1979]
69–71), Best analyzes Smith's secret Mark (pp. 71–76).

[8]"Clement of Alexandria: A Review of Research," *Second
Century* 4 (1983) 219–44.

[9]"On the Mar Saba Letter Attributed to Clement of Alexandria," *Journal of Early Christian Studies* 3 (1995) 216.

[10]Other challenges to the authenticity of the secret gospel
include discussions by J. A. Fitzmyer in "How to Exploit a Secret
Gospel," *America* (June 23, 1973) 570–72; H. Merkel, "Auf den
Spuren des Urmarkus? Ein neuer Fund und seine Beurteilung,"
Zeitschrift für Theologie und Kirche 71 (1974) 123–44; and Murgia in

of any physical tests made of the handwriting that Smith edited; an analysis of the chemical composition of the ink could be used to compare it to inks characteristic of given periods. It would also be important to know whether there are other handwritten notes in the book containing the fragment of Clement, but Smith never discussed the point—and no other Western scholar has ever seen the volume![11]

In view of such desiderata, as yet unfulfilled, as well as the implications of the statistical analyses made by Best and by Criddle, it is not surprising that legitimate doubts continue to persist concerning the authenticity of the document edited by Smith.

The Partridge Manuscript

When I first made the acquaintance of the learned and kindly Dr. William H. P. Hatch in the 1940s, I was unaware that several years earlier he had been deceived by a well-planned hoax involving a fake New Testament manuscript. It was only at a later time that I began to hear occasional rumors about the production of a parchment leaf, inscribed by two students at the Episcopal Theological School in

---

response to R. H. Fuller's "Longer Mark: Forgery, Interpolation, or Old Tradition?" in *Protocol of the 18th Colloquy of the Center for Hermeneutical Studies* (ed. W. Wuellner; Berkeley, Calif.: The Center, 1976). Murgia argues (pp. 35–40) that the letter is intended to provide a bogus seal of authenticity for the secret gospel, and that the absence of major textual errors implies that the manuscript edited by Smith is probably an original composition rather than the product of repeated copying.

[11]In 1980 while visiting Mar Saba monastery, Thomas J. Talley was told that the book had been removed to the library of the Greek Patriarch in Jerusalem; see Talley's comments in his paper "Liturgical Time in the Ancient Church," in *Liturgical Time: Papers Read at the 1981 Congress of the Societas Liturgica* (ed. W. Vos and G. Wainwright; Rotterdam: Liturgical Ecumenical Center Trust, 1982) 45.

Cambridge, Massachusetts. The full story of their escapade is a classic and deserves to be retold.[12]

In 1936 Professor Norman Nash, a colleague of Dr. Hatch, was explaining to the junior class in New Testament Studies that scholars for some time had been struck by the curious construction of the fifteenth chapter of Paul's Epistle to the Romans. He indicated that he had come to feel that the doxology appearing in Romans 16:25–27 was originally to be found between verses 13 and 14 of the fifteenth chapter. Nash acknowledged that there was no manuscript evidence that supported his theory, but he concluded, "Who knows what archaeologists may one day turn up?"

Following the class Barrett Tyler and Reamer Kline talked further about their professor's wistful comment. Between the two of them they formed a plan to provide what Nash was hoping would some day turn up. At one of the stationery shops on Harvard Square they obtained a sheet of high-grade parchment. After returning to their room in Lawrence Hall they proceeded to "age" their purchase in a solution of coffee grounds and strong tea. Following repeated boilings and soakings the desired coloration was achieved and the now antiqued parchment was placed under the dormitory doormat, where the traffic of students' feet would give the sheet a still more aged appearance.

By practicing with a broad-nib pen, Kline copied on ordinary paper the style of Greek script from photostats of various New Testament Greek manuscripts. Finally he chose the fourth-century Codex Vaticanus as his model. This is written in uncial letters, the capital letters of the Greek alphabet, and therefore the easiest ancient style to imitate. Beginning with Romans chapter 15, as precisely as possible Kline copied the text of Vaticanus until he came to verse 14.

---

[12]The account given here is a condensation (permission granted) of an article that appeared in *Yankee* magazine for December, 1974, entitled "The Great Manuscript Hoax," written by the Reverend Stephen K. Jackson, Rector of St. Mary's Episcopal Church, Manchester, Connecticut.

There he inserted the "missing" doxology and continued on to the end of the page.

Next it was necessary to bring the "Kline-Taylor manuscript" to the attention of New Testament scholars. A letter was written on stationery from the Hotel Essex near South Station in Boston and sent to Professor Nash. It read as follows:

April 27, 1936

Dear Professor Nash,

Enclosed you will find a manuscript which I bought during a recent trip in Egypt. I happened to be staying in Cairo and visited my friend Howard Lowell. While I was showing him various curios collected during the trip he became particularly interested in this manuscript.

I called your house this morning but you were out. I am leaving for Portland on business but will stop on my way back. I would appreciate any information you might give me concerning this manuscript as to whether it might be of value. Looking forward to meeting you, I remain very truly yours,

Wilfred J. Partridge

229 Greenwood Boulevard
Evanston, Illinois

The letter and the manuscript arrived in the office of Professor Nash two days later. Being a cautious man by nature, Nash was skeptical but intrigued. It had the feel of an ancient manuscript, and important discoveries have occasionally happened unexpectedly. At any rate, he was certain that his colleague, Will Hatch, an internationally recognized authority on uncial manuscripts, could give an authoritative opinion about the value of the manuscript. Professor Hatch enthusiastically agreed to offer an opinion concerning the authenticity and value of the fragment.

The style of the script was clearly similar to that of other fourth-century specimens. After consultation with Professor Gulick of Harvard it seemed that the manuscript warranted serious consideration. The unexpected location of the doxology stimulated additional attention, and a technical opinion was requested from the Fogg Museum. The Fogg specialists asked for permission to scrape off a bit of ink for chemical analysis. Apart from such an analysis, they could render only a tentative opinion that the ink appeared to be of a variety common to many ancient manuscripts.

Nash and Hatch agreed that chemical analysis was called for but were reluctant to go ahead with it without first receiving permission from the owner of the document. Unfortunately, Mr. Partridge of Evanston, Illinois, had not returned from his business trip and consequently was unavailable.

The Episcopal Theological School is a small community and interest in the Partridge Fragment began to spread. At this point Tyler and Kline began to have second thoughts. Their "fragment" had been taken seriously and academic reputations were at stake. Their own academic future could be in some jeopardy.

A few days later a postcard arrived at Professor Nash's office with a Cambridge postmark and dated April 30. It contained an adapted quotation from Lewis Carroll's *Through the Looking-Glass* and was signed by the missing Wilfred J. Partridge. It read,

"The time has come," the Walrus said,
"To talk of many things:
Of manuscripts and sealing wax—
Of cabbages—and kings—."

The following day the two students appeared in Nash's office and revealed the entire story to him. An unamused Professor Hatch was informed as gently as possible, and the "Partridge Fragment" was retrieved from the Fogg Museum.

Tyler and Kline were graduated in 1938 and were subsequently ordained in the Episcopal Church. Kline went on to become president of Bard College at Annandale-on-Hudson, and Tyler became a military chaplain. Professor Hatch never quite got over his sense of professional embarrassment, and the Partridge Fragment was rarely mentioned in his presence.

Ten years later, in 1948, a magnificent stained glass window was dedicated at Episcopal Theological School in memory of Barrett Tyler, who had been killed in the service of his country in World War II. The circular window depicts scenes from *Pilgrim's Progress* and contains an inconspicuous memento recollecting the hoax of the Wilfred Partridge manuscript. The central panel shows Bunyan's Christian, at whose feet stands the figure of a partridge, firmly grasping a cord from which dangles a rolled scroll!

Following the ceremony of dedication of the window Hatch was heard to say that he could not recall the mention of a bird in Bunyan's classic allegory. Whether anyone ventured to explain to him the reason for its presence in the window must remain unknown.

An Amusing Agraphon

Fortunately the students' hoax of the Partridge manuscript had not reached the stage of publication, but another hoax (as I regard it) was eventually published in an altogether respectable biblical quarterly.

As was mentioned earlier in chapter 2, my supervisor for Ph.D. work in classics at Princeton University was Paul R. Coleman-Norton. A cosmopolitan and urbane associate professor of Latin, he was accustomed to enliven his classes with an occasional wisecrack or humorous anecdote. I recall that on one occasion he told the class about the query of someone who had been puzzled by Jesus' announcement that the wicked would suffer amid weeping and gnashing of teeth. "But Master," asked a disciple, "what if a man has no teeth?" The response of Jesus was: "Teeth will be provided." With this as background, let me condense the content of an article that Coleman-Norton submitted to several different journals.

In June of 1942, Coleman-Norton undertook military duty and was stationed in French Morocco of North Africa at the town of Fédhala. Here his assignment involved American censorship specializing in control of prisoner-of-war information. In the autumn of 1943 he had opportunity to visit the town's only Mohammedan mosque. Here the imam showed him, among other things, a thick tome composed almost entirely of Arabic writings. In this volume was a single unnumbered page of Greek text sandwiched between two tractates on *materia medica* attributed to the celebrated Arabian physician and philosopher, commonly known as Avicenna. On a subsequent visit to the mosque Coleman-Norton was given permission by the imam to copy the Greek text of the leaf.

Upon his release from the United States Army in February 1946, Coleman-Norton resumed his academic routine and had time for pursuing projects of research. One of the latter was further study of the copy he had made of the Greek text. It turned out, he said, to be the sole surviving copy of a Greek translation of a portion of the Latin *Opus Imperfectum in Matthaeum*. This is a collection of fifty-four homilies constructed in the form of a commentary on the Gospel according to Matthew (chapters 1–13 and 19–25), once ascribed to the authorship of St. John Chrysostom, bishop of Constantinople, but now commonly considered anonymous. What was especially noteworthy was the presence of a hitherto unknown saying attributed to Jesus following the reference to "weeping and gnashing of teeth" in 24:51. This *agraphon* (as such extra-canonical sayings of Jesus are called) is absent from the Latin text of the *Opus Imperfectum* and is without parallel in patristic literature. The English translation of the *agraphon,* made by Coleman-Norton, is as follows:

> And behold, a certain one of his disciples standing by said unto him, "Rabbi" (which is to say, being interpreted, Master), "how can these things be, if they are toothless?" And Jesus answered and said, "O thou of little faith, trouble not thyself; if haply they will be lacking any, teeth will be provided."

Following the *agraphon* was an extended discussion (some twenty-two lines) by the author of the *Opus Imperfectum*. With great erudition Coleman-Norton prepared a scholarly commentary on the Greek text of the discussion. He pointed out instances in the text of *figurae etymologicae,* chiasmus, crassis, elision, and asyndeton—all of which he was accustomed to use in his own writing. The entire article was furnished with numerous footnotes, in one of which Coleman-Norton acknowledges my help in providing information from A. S. Lewis's volume on the Sinaitic Syriac Palimpsest.

Coleman-Norton submitted his article for publication in the *Harvard Theological Review.* Its editor, Arthur Darby Nock, wrote to me inquiring who Coleman-Norton was, since he had never seen any contribution by him in theological journals. Since Nock mentioned something of the content of Coleman-Norton's article, I reported that *prior* to the Second World War I had been present in his class when he told a witticism about "teeth will be provided."

Nock responded to Coleman-Norton that he would publish the article if he could supply a photograph of the parchment leaf. Coleman-Norton replied that he had indeed attempted to obtain such a photograph but that he could not do so, for the area in which the mosque was located had been posted off limits to Allied personnel because a recent incident had caused "bad blood" between the residents and the Americans.

After Nock returned the article, Coleman-Norton submitted it to the *Journal of Biblical Literature.* The editor, Philip Hyatt of Vanderbilt University, wrote to me asking essentially the same question that Nock had asked, and I responded as I had done earlier. After Hyatt returned the manuscript, Coleman-Norton sent it to the *Journal of Religion,* published by the University of Chicago Press. Amos Wilder, the editor at that time, may have inquired about Coleman-Norton, or he may have assessed the article on its own merits. At any rate, the manuscript must have been returned, for eventually it was published in the *Catholic Biblical Quarterly.*[13]

---

[13] "An Amusing Agraphon," 12 (1950) 439–49.

Coleman-Norton subsequently told me that he was quite unhappy about the manner in which the article was printed. Instead of maintaining the lineation of the Greek text as it was presented in the typescript, the compositor, perhaps in order to save space, set the material in a broader column and, as a result, cross-references from the commentary to lines in the Greek text are altogether inexact.

Since it seemed to me to be a delicate subject to broach to my former graduate supervisor, I never ventured to question Coleman-Norton concerning the authenticity of the alleged leaf of Greek text. However, from my having taken two lecture courses in patristics from him, as well as a course in Greek composition, I was well acquainted with his penchant for telling all kinds of jokes and witticisms. Consequently, I am convinced that his article, "An Amusing Agraphon," is a *pia fraus.*

Chapter 12

VEXATIONS OF AN AUTHOR

THE feeling of satisfaction at having finished writing the manuscript of a book or an article is sometimes replaced later by chagrin at finding typographical errors in what has come from the press. Those who have read proof can resonate with the following anonymous doggerel:

> The typographical error is a slippery thing and sly.
> You can hunt till you are dizzy, but somehow it will get by.
> 'Til the forms are off the presses, it is strange how still it keeps.
> It shrinks down in the corner, and it never stirs or peeps.
> The typographical error is too small for human eyes
> 'Til the ink is on the paper, when it grows to mountain size.
> The boss just stares with horror, then he grabs his hair and groans.
> The copy reader drops her head upon her hands and moans.
> The remainder of the issue may be clean as clean can be,
> But the typographical error is the only thing you sea!

Especially vexatious is the creation of a typographical error by the press after the author had approved the correct final page proof. In my book *The Text of the New Testament,* I described the text of Melchiorre Sessa's edition of the Greek New Testament (Venice 1538) as "curiously eclectic." When the book was published in 1964 one can imagine my chagrin (not to say shock!) to read that Sessa's text was "curiously electric"—and this in spite of the final proof of this page having the correct reading.[1]

How it happened that the word was altered is a mystery. C. H. Roberts, secretary to the delegates of Oxford Press, suggested that the pressman may have accidentally dropped the form thereby dislocating the page, and then, instead of sending it back to the composing room, attempted to set it right himself—with unhappy consequences.

On another occasion I was invited by the editor of *Religious Studies News* to prepare for the September 1994 issue a memorial notice of the death of Professor Kurt Aland, a long-time friend and colleague. Naturally I spent a considerable amount of time in preparing what I thought would be a worthy account in an article entitled "Kurt Aland: In Memoriam."

When the article was published, however, I was embarrassed to find a half-dozen typographical errors, including the omission of two prepositions that were needed for the sense. My earlier request to be allowed to see a proof of the piece could not be granted, I was told, because during August the office force of Scholars Press would be on holiday.

Still more vexatious was the discovery on two other occasions that changes had been made deliberately in articles I had submitted—changes that modified significantly the meaning of what I had written. In one case the change was discovered in the proof stage and could therefore be rectified. This involved the article on Kirsopp Lake that I had been invited to prepare for *The Dictionary of American Biography*.[2] In my research prior to writing the article I sought, and received, personal information from Lake's daughter, Agnes K. Lake Michels, at that time professor of Latin at Bryn Mawr College. In the article I tried to give a

---

[1] *The Text of the New Testament: Its Transmission, Corruption, and Restoration* (Oxford: Clarendon) 103.

[2] *Supplement* 4 (ed. J. A. Garraty and E. T. James; New York: Scribner's, 1974) 467–69.

balanced evaluation of Lake as a New Testament scholar, and I concluded with the statement: "His studies on St. Paul and primitive Christianity, though brilliant in their assessment of the influence of the Graeco-Roman background on the early church, gave insufficient attention (as was true of other New Testament research during the first third of the twentieth century) to the Jewish milieu from which Christianity and important New Testament documents emerged." When I received the page proofs, I found that my evaluation had been recast so that it now contained only positive, laudatory statements about Lake's contributions as a scholar.

I wrote at once to the editor stating that unless what I had originally submitted were restored, I did not want my name to stand at the close of the article as author. Happily, when the volume was published in 1974, the account was printed as I had originally written it. I never learned how it had come about that my assessment was rewritten.

In another case of unauthorized change, however, correction was not made until several years following the publication of the printed volume. I had been invited to contribute fifteen articles to *Collier's Encyclopedia,*[3] a general reference work of some twenty volumes. Among the several editors of the encyclopedia, two were assigned to give attention to articles that dealt with religious subjects. One editor was my former professor of church history, Dr. Frederick W. Loetscher, and the other was the Reverend Robert I. Gannon, S.J. The intention of the publishers was to have the articles written by Protestant authors examined for balance and impartiality by Father Gannon, and the articles written by Roman Catholic authors examined by Dr. Loetscher. In either case, modifications introduced by an editor were to be submitted to the original author for final approval or further emendation.

At the close of my article on "New Testament" I had originally written:

---

[3]New York: Collier, 1957.

No council recognized by all Churches has ever made a pronouncement on the limits of the canon. The Council of Trent, in 1546, explicitly defined them for Roman Catholics, and the encyclical "Providentissimus Deus" (1893) explained in Roman Catholic terms the belief, which is common to all Christians, that the canonical books are divinely inspired.

When the volume was published, however, I found that I was made to say that only the Roman Catholic Church holds that the Bible is divinely inspired. At once I wrote to the editor-in-chief of the encyclopedia, detailing my grievance and expressing a lack of confidence that what was attributed to other authors of signed articles had been actually written by them. My concluding sentence—"It is difficult for me to regard the Collier's Encyclopedia as an impartial authority in articles on religion, nor do I see how I can continue to recommend it to my students either for consultation or for purchase"—brought at once an apology from the editor and the assurance that he knew of only one other instance where a similar situation had arisen. The letter concluded with the promise that in the next printing my original statement would be restored to the article. Dr. Loetscher subsequently informed me that he had sent all articles written by Protestant authors for inspection by Father Gannon, but that Gannon sent no articles to him.

Other vexations arise because of delay in publication. Such postponement is especially irksome when a terminal date is mentioned in the title, as was the case with my "Classified Bibliography of the Graeco-Roman Mystery Religions, 1924–1973." In the early 1970s I had been asked by Wolfgang Haase of Tübingen to prepare a bibliography on the mystery religions for inclusion in the volume on pagan religions for the series *Aufstieg und Niedergang der römischen Welt.* Since there had been a notable increase during the previous half-century in the number of publications bearing on the ancient mystery religions, it seemed appropriate to focus on that period—hence the dates mentioned in the title.

As it turned out, however, several of the other authors solicited by Haase were dilatory in submitting the articles they had agreed to prepare. Five years after I had submitted my article, Haase wrote to me suggesting that, in view of the delay, I should prepare a supplement, bringing the bibliography up to date. Despite the inconvenience (and tedium) of searching once again through a wide variety of periodicals, I collected additional information that increased the sum total of items in the bibliography from 3,170 items to 3,647, and the title was modified by the addition of the words "With a Supplement, 1974–1977."

Unhappily, the publication of the volume was delayed for several more years, and Haase once again wrote to inquire whether I would prepare another supplement. This time, however, I responded that other literary commitments would prevent my doing so. Actually, it was chiefly that I could not face the dreary prospect of undertaking yet again a comprehensive search. Eventually, in 1984, ten years after I had sent the major part of the bibliography, de Gruyter published the long-delayed volume, with my bibliography of 160 pages standing first in the volume.

Still more vexatious was another case that involved multiple delays in publication. The introduction to my *Annotated Bibliography of the Textual Criticism of the New Testament, 1914–1939* concludes with the succinct statement: "Although the material for this volume was ready for the press eight years ago, for various reasons beyond my control its appearance has been greatly delayed."[4] The story of the many and varied delays is almost beyond belief.

It was in mid-1945 that I submitted the manuscript of an annotated bibliography on New Testament textual criticism to Silva Lake for possible inclusion in Studies and Documents, a series that Kirsopp Lake and she had founded the previous decade. Early in 1946 Mrs. Lake wrote saying that she would publish the bibliography if I were able to obtain a grant-in-aid of publication from the American Council of Learned Societies. "Of course," she continued, "if you found

---

[4] Studies and Documents 16 (Copenhagen: E. Munksgaard, 1955) ix.

someone to undertake publication immediately, without waiting for the decision of the ACLS, you probably should accept it. I, however, feel fairly sure that we can find the money somewhere else if they turn us down."

I promptly made application to the ACLS for a grant. After several months of waiting I received a response from the secretary for fellowships and grants, stating that "because of circumstances beyond the control of the Council it is not probable that applications for subventions in support of grants for publication can be acted upon before the late autumn of 1946."

As it turned out, however, it was not until September of 1947 that I received application forms from the council, which I was asked to fill out in duplicate. After mailing them back to the council I learned that the wrong forms had been mistakenly sent to me, and another set needed to be submitted; this set required Mrs. Lake's attention as well as information that I was asked to provide. Because of illness, however, Mrs. Lake was unable to return her form to me until December; of course I sent it on promptly to the American Council.

Six months later, Mrs. Lake's next letter to me contained the welcome information that a few weeks earlier she had received notice from the council that it would grant the five hundred dollars that had been requested. She apologized for the delay in writing me and explained that it was

> because I was quite ill at the time that I received your last letter, and then suddenly received the offer of a teaching position at Occidental College [in Los Angeles], which took all the slight strength I had for the first few months. Now, however, I am completely recovered.
>
> In a few days I shall send you your manuscript for final proof-reading. . . . As soon as you return it to me it can go to the Waverly Press [in Baltimore].

I waited in vain for the promised return of the manuscript. It was a year and a half later before I had any further communication from Mrs. Lake. This was in December

1950 while both of us were attending the annual meeting in New York of the Society of Biblical Literature. It was then I learned that the Waverly Press was not accepting additional manuscripts for the Studies and Documents series, and that through her new co-editor, Carsten Høeg, future mono-graphs of the series would be printed by the firm of Munks-gaard in Copenhagen. She said that proofs of my book would be arriving shortly.

After the lapse of seven months without receiving any further information or proofs, I wrote to Høeg directly. At the end of August 1951 he responded saying that he had learned rather incidentally from the printing house that the first fifty or so pages of my book were in proof. He contin-ued: "I did not know a word about it; she had apparently sent the MS directly to the printer. I told them to stop printing until I could get in touch with Mrs. Lake and obtain the necessary information. . . . Meanwhile, I send you the proofs without delay in spite of the fact that I have not read them myself. When you have read them, I ask you to return them to me; I hope in the meantime the situation may be clarified."

Four months later Høeg wrote as follows:

> I still have not got a letter from Mrs. Lake and I am more and more embarrassed. I understand that the American Council has granted the sum necessary for printing of the book and consequently we could finish the printing here and, I assume, get the money directly from the American Council. The trouble is that we have not got the rest of the manuscript. *If* you have got a double of your manuscript, and *if* you will have the trouble to go it through and bring it in perfect accordance with the [edited] manuscript which was used by the printer for the first pages, and *if* the American Council will give its consent, I will gladly take the responsibility of issuing the book, of course as part of "Studies and Documents." Please write me and inform me of your intentions.

Unfortunately, I possessed no carbon copy of the manuscript because over the years, as additional items came to my attention, I would paste insertions here and there throughout the pages of the manuscript. Happily, I had had a microfilm made of the completed text just before mailing it to Mrs. Lake. As a last resort, therefore, I could employ someone to prepare a new typescript from the last two-thirds of the microfilm.

Before doing that, I decided to make one more effort to secure the return of the manuscript itself. Among the students at Princeton Seminary was a Californian named David Weatherford, a graduate of Occidental College where Mrs. Lake was teaching. In consultation with him I learned that he was planning to return to California during the Christmas holiday and would very likely see Mrs. Lake when he visited a college friend who was staying in Mrs. Lake's home as a lodger.

Accordingly, I wrote again to Mrs. Lake indicating that I had a number of additional bibliographical items that I wished to insert into the latter part of my manuscript. "In case you have not yet shipped it to me," I wrote, "you may give it to David Weatherford, who plans to visit you during the holiday season. He can bring it back to Princeton with him and thus save you the trouble of wrapping it up for the Express Company."

Early in 1952, after the close of the Christmas holiday I was, of course, eager to learn what success Weatherford may have had. Alas! he returned without the manuscript. He reported that when he had asked Mrs. Lake for the material, she put him off, saying that the manuscript was apart in various rooms in her house, and that she would shortly be assembling it and returning it to Metzger.

Still another worrisome problem arose when I received a letter in April from the executive director of the American Council of Learned Societies, Charles E. Odegaard, who wrote as follows:

> I can imagine how annoyed you must be over the publication history of your volume in the *Studies and Documents* series. Like others, we in the ACLS have been unable to get any information out of Mrs. Lake and I have abandoned the effort

to deal with her. I talked with Carsten Høeg in Paris in February and told him that if he would write me a letter stating where the volume now stands in terms of its publication history in Denmark under his auspices and if he assures me by letter that the volume can now be published in Denmark, I will then feel free to turn over to him the $500 subsidy; though technically the Council's obligation in this respect is terminated by virtue of failure to publish within the originally agreed upon time. We cannot keep postponing forever the subsidy, and it will revert if we are not assured before long that actual publication is imminent. I am not saying this to upset you, but merely to indicate that I am especially anxious to hear from Høeg so we can terminate this matter.

At once I set about to find a graduate student in New Testament who might wish to earn some extra money by preparing a typescript of the last two-thirds of the microfilm. Fortunately one of the New Testament doctoral students, Roy Harrisville, indicated that he would have time to undertake the onerous task during the spring of 1952.

After the typing had been completed, it took me several days in proofreading the manuscript and conforming its style to that of the first fifty pages now in printer's proof. Inasmuch as in June I would be attending a meeting of British and American members of the International Greek New Testament Project (see pp. 62–63 above), I wrote to Høeg indicating that following the meeting I would be able to go on to Copenhagen in order to deliver the newly prepared manuscript to him in person. As it turned out, however, Høeg was to be in Brussels at that time attending sessions of the Union académique internationale. He suggested that I meet him there.

Consequently, following the meeting in Oxford, I found my way to the Palais de l'Académie, where Høeg was scheduled to report on his progress in editing several magnificent volumes of *Monumenta Musicae Byzantinae*. Later, at Høeg's suggestion the chairman of the session on "Instrumenta" invited me to make a report about the ongoing work of the International Greek New Testament Project, which I did. It goes without saying that I was happy to turn over to Høeg the rest of the manuscript of my bibliography.

There was, however, yet another kind of delay that postponed publication once again. Shortly after I had returned to Princeton and Høeg had delivered the material to the firm of Munksgaard (which was also the printer of the volumes on Byzantine music), all the printers in Denmark went on strike for higher wages. Negotiations dragged on and on. Finally a settlement was reached, and in due course I received the proofs of the rest of my book.

Eventually, after so many and such varied kinds of delays, the book was published in 1955 as volume 16 of the Studies and Documents series—exactly ten years after the material had been submitted.

Finally, I mention yet another instance in which, as it seemed, the plans of author or editor would be frustrated and come to naught. In the late 1950s the idea occurred to me that there was need for the creation of a series of monographs that would include critical studies as well as tools for the study of the New Testament—such as bibliographies, concordances, and the like. The name I proposed for the series was "New Testament Tools and Studies." Among the volumes I thought might be included in the series were a bibliography of periodical literature on the Apostle Paul that I had begun to assemble, a concordance to the distinctive Greek text of Codex Bezae that a doctoral student of mine had compiled in preparation for writing his dissertation, and a collection of my own articles on the history of New Testament textual criticism.

One publishing house after another did not see its way clear to launching a series that would sometimes include volumes of interest to only a narrow range of prospective purchasers. After exhausting my list of publishers in the United States that I thought might conceivably take on the series, I solicited several in Great Britain and in Germany. As the writer of Proverbs declares,

"Hope deferred makes the heart sick"—and I experienced disappointment twelve times.

The thirteenth publisher that I approached was E. J. Brill of Leiden. Founded in 1683, the firm of Brill is one of the oldest publishing houses in the world and is the oldest independent publisher in the Netherlands. Its list of publications comprises books, reference works, and about thirty journals for the specialist scholarly market, mainly in the humanities and with particular emphasis on the classical tradition, intellectual history, and religion. One can imagine my feeling of elation when I received word from the director, Mr. F. C. Wieder, Jr., informing me that Brill would indeed undertake to issue the series. He would not, he wrote, require a subvention to help defray the expense of typesetting of any volume (something that I had begun, rather rashly, to offer as an inducement to prospective publishers—though where I would be able to find money for such subvention I did not know!); nor, on the other hand, would Brill promise to pay any royalties to author or editor for volumes that appeared in the series.

On a subsequent visit to Holland I made a point of going to the printing house and making personal acquaintance with Mr. Wieder. I was impressed by the beehive of activity in progress on the premises of the firm, which proudly identifies itself as "Publisher of the Learned World." One artisan was setting up Chinese characters by hand, perhaps for the distinguished journal of Sinology, *T'oung Pao,* then well into its second century of publication; another was composing in Arabic a monthly publication to be distributed in Cairo, Egypt; still others were busying themselves at other workplaces throughout the floor.

After thirty years of editing the series, in 1993, following the publication of volume 15, I decided to seek a younger scholar who might be persuaded to join me as co-editor. Happily a former student of mine, Bart Ehrman, associate professor of religious studies at the University of North Carolina at Chapel Hill, agreed to take on this responsibility, and the last six volumes now carry both our names as editors. There was also a welcome offer on the part of the current director of the series, Dr. David Orton, that Brill henceforth would provide annually a small stipend to each editor in order to cover expenses of postage in sending manuscripts between editors and authors and publisher.

*   *   *   *

The preceding account of instances involving vexation may give the impression that I have lived in an almost constant state of distress and grievance. That is not true. On the contrary, I have pleasant recollections of many, many instances of satisfaction and appreciation for positive relationships that I have enjoyed over the years with publishers, editors, and copy-readers. In fact, when I survey the circumstances that brought about temporary vexation, a comment made in Virgil's *Aeneid* (1.203) comes to mind:

> *Forsan et haec olim meminisse iuvabit.*
> (Perhaps someday it will be gratifying
> to recall even these [distresses].)

~~~ Chapter 13 ~~~

PROJECTS AND MISSIONS

O NE of the bibliographical projects that I launched
in the 1940s was the compilation of an index of
articles on the New Testament and the early church
published in Festschriften. The practice of assembling and
publishing a Festschrift has been a pleasant way of acknowl-
edging publically the contributions to scholarship made by
the person to whom the volume is dedicated. The negative
side, however, of writing an article for such a volume has
often been recognized—as, for example, F. F. Bruce comments in his autobiography:

> Back in my Cambridge days Peter Giles, Master of Em-
> manuel College, used to tell us that any scholar who wrote
> an article for a Festschrift might as well dig a hole in his
> back garden and bury it, for in a year or two it would be
> forgotten and there would be no convenient means of
> recording its existence.[1]

Professor Bruce's account of Giles's pessimistic evaluation of Festschriften in the early thirties continues as follows:

> The situation is a little better now with modern means of
> indexing: I have found very useful, for example, an *Index of
> Articles on the New Testament and the Early Church Published in
> Festschriften,* compiled in 1951 by Bruce M. Metzger (with a
> supplement published in 1955).[2]

---

[1]*In Retrospect: Remembrance of Things Past* (Grand Rapids,
Mich.: Eerdmans, 1980) 276.
[2]Ibid.

In compiling the index mentioned by Professor Bruce, I was led in my pursuit of fugitive Festschriften beyond the field of New Testament into such fields as ancient art and archaeology, Byzantine research, the classics, Egyptology, English literature, intertestamental literature, Judaica, the mystery cults, mythology, coins, Oriental languages and literatures, palaeography, papyrology, patristics, philology in general, philosophy, and theology in general. Of more than twelve hundred Festschriften that I located in the twelve libraries that I visited here and abroad, nearly six hundred contained a total of twenty-one hundred articles bearing on the New Testament and the early church. These I classified under a broad schema, and also provided an index of the authors of articles.

In 1951 the Society of Biblical Literature published my index as volume 5 of its newly established Monograph Series. Because the book contained 182 pages, the editor of the series, Ralph Marcus of the University of Chicago, thought it necessary to provide the following preliminary note for my camera-ready typescript:

> The editorial committee of the Society of Biblical Literature feels that to the prevailing rule of publishing monographs not exceeding 125 pages some exceptions should be made from time to time. We feel that the present monograph has deservedly been made such an exception.[3]

The rule Marcus refers to had no doubt been formulated in view of the limited funds available for issuing such volumes. In my case a contract was drawn up stating that I would pay for the cost of publishing but that as copies were sold an equivalent amount (but no more) would eventually be refunded to me.

Tracking Down New Testament Manuscripts

Over the years the number of known New Testament Greek manuscripts keeps increasing as additional examples

---

[3] *Index of Articles on the New Testament and the Early Church Published in Festschriften* (Philadelphia, Pa.).

come to light. The first New Testament papyrus became available in 1868, when Constantin Tischendorf published a seventh-century fragment containing sixty-two verses of 1 Corinthians (now designated $\mathfrak{P}^{11}$). By 1994 Kurt Aland, who had been keeping the official register of all known New Testament Greek manuscripts, was able to list ninety-nine Greek papyri.

The number of parchment manuscripts of the New Testament has also been increasing. In 1963 Aland could list 250 uncial manuscripts and 2,646 minuscule manuscripts; by 1994 the numbers had risen to 306 and 2,856. In a very minor way I contributed by bringing to Aland's attention four manuscripts for inclusion in the official listing.

In 1952 I was invited to teach for a term at the Seminario Teológico Presbiteriano at Campinas, Brazil. Several months prior to leaving for South America I wrote to twelve libraries and museums in Brazil, Argentina, and Chile, inquiring whether they possessed any Greek manuscripts of the New Testament. In response I received replies from four institutions, only one of which indicated there was a Greek manuscript among the holdings of the Biblioteca Nacional in Rio de Janeiro. The librarian, however, confessed that he was unable to identify the contents of the manuscript.

At a suitable time during my stay in Campinas I travelled to Rio and asked for permission to examine the manuscript. It turned out to be a parchment codex of the four Gospels, measuring twenty-one by fifteen cm, with one column of writing per page. The manuscript originally contained 234 folios; the first ten folios were missing, and the text of Matthew began at 9:17. On the basis of the style of script I judged that the manuscript was written perhaps in the twelfth century.

I was told that the library had received the manuscript June 24, 1912, from the estate of Dr. João Pandiá Cológeras. Consulting A.V.A. Sacramento Blake's *Diccionario bibliográphica brazileiro*[4] I discovered that Cológeras had founded at Petrópolis a primary and secondary school and was the author of several books. His father had been born in Corfu and probably brought the manuscript with him when he came to Brazil.

After returning to the United States I sent Professor Aland palaeographical information about the manuscript, to which he assigned the official number 2437. As of 1994 it was still the only Greek New Testament manuscript in Central and South America included in his list.

Another opportunity of tracking down manuscripts of the Greek New Testament came in the mid-eighties while I was on a lecture tour in South Africa. Before leaving I happened to read in the April 1985 issue of the *South African Panorama* an interesting article entitled "Medieval Treasures." This was a description of medieval and Renaissance manuscripts bequeathed by the former British governor of the Cape of Good Hope, Sir George Grey, to the South African Library in Cape Town. Most of the manuscripts were Latin, but the article also made a brief reference to a Greek Gospel book. This attracted my interest, and while spending several days lecturing at the University of Cape Town, I visited the library.

The librarian in charge of special collections informed me that the library actually possessed two Greek manuscripts, and brought out both of them for my examination. One of the two, identified by the shelf mark 4C1, has 291 folios and measures 31.4 by 23.7 cm. Each folio of rather coarse parchment contains two columns of twenty lines each. The style of the minuscule Greek hand suggests that it was written in the twelfth century. The text of the Gospels is arranged in accord with the typical Byzantine Greek lectionary, with the menologion beginning on folio 193.

The other manuscript, with the shelf mark 4C6, is of medium fine quality of parchment, and originally had 223 folios, but now lacks the first thirty-two. Each folio measures 30.9 by 22.9 cm and is written in two columns of twenty-four lines each. According to a colophon on the last

---

[4]Rio de Janeiro: Typographia Nacional, 1883–1902.

folio the scribe was a priest in Crete named Nikolas who finished copying the manuscript August 12, 1269. The colophon also pronounces an anathema upon anyone who might steal the manuscript. The text is arranged in accord with the typical Byzantine Greek lectionary, with the menologion beginning on folio 151.

After returning to the United States, I sent Aland palaeographical information about the two manuscripts; he assigned to manuscript 4C1 the official siglum *l* 2279, and to manuscript 4C6, the siglum *l* 2280. As of 1994 these are the only Greek New Testament manuscripts that have been reported in Africa, with the exception of several in Egypt.

On another occasion, and without travelling beyond the university library in Princeton, I was able to direct scholarly attention to the existence (and the publication) of a fifth-century fragment of the Letter to Titus. It was while I was going through thousands of volumes of journals and serials of all kinds in order to collect material for my *Annotated Bibliography of the Textual Criticism of the New Testament* that I came upon a puzzling title of an article in the publications of the Académie royale de Belgique for 1932. This was an article by the Georgian scholar G. Zereteli with the title, "Un palimpseste grec du Vᵉ siècle sur parchemin (Epist. ad Fit. 1.4–6, 7–9)."[5] When I investigated the article I found that "Fit." was a typographical error and that the existence of a New Testament fragment had been overlooked by von Dobschütz and his successors who were keeping the official listing of all New Testament manuscripts.

Consequently I drew up a brief note entitled "A Hitherto Neglected Early Fragment of the Epistle to Titus," and submitted it to the newly established journal, *Novum Testamentum*, where it was published in volume 1.[6] An offprint of the article that I sent to Dr. Erwin Nestle brought

---

[5] *Académie royale de Belgique, Bulletin de la classe des Lettres,* Vᵉ sér., 18, 427–32.

[6] *Novum Testamentum* (1956) 149–50.

back a postcard congratulating me upon having rescued the fragment from oblivion.

A Concordance to the Syriac New Testament

In the early 1960s Ernest Colwell, at that time president of the Southern California School of Theology, received a letter from a certain Mrs. Bonus of Burnham-on-Crouch in England. She informed him that in 1926 her late husband's uncle, the Reverend Albert Bonus of Alphington, Exeter, had finished compiling a concordance to the Peshitta Syriac New Testament, and that it was now in her possession. She called it an objet d'art, since the concordance was entirely in his handwriting, and inquired of Colwell how much he would offer her for it.

Colwell, knowing that I was to make a trip that summer to England on behalf of the International Greek New Testament Project, asked me whether I would pay Mrs. Bonus a visit in order to examine the concordance. I agreed to do so, thinking that perhaps Bonus's work could be published in my newly established series, New Testament Tools and Studies.

At the appointed time I arrived at Mrs. Bonus's home and found that she had arranged for her lawyer to be present while I examined portions of the manuscript. It comprised about six hundred sheets of foolscap, each with three columns of neatly written Syriac lemmata. The concordance seemed to be a competent piece of scholarly work, but to assess its monetary value in terms of its being an objet d'art, as Mrs. Bonus wished to do, was to confuse the usefulness of a scholarly tool with something of a totally different genre.

The result of my visit was a disappointment to Mrs. Bonus and, to a lesser extent, to me as well. I was unable to suggest to her any academic institution that would be likely to pay the amount that she seemed to have in mind for her artistic treasure. Nevertheless, I assured Mrs. Bonus that I would report to Dr. Colwell and that an attempt would be made to find a purchaser of the manuscript. For my part, I noticed that here and there Bonus had written in the margin a stray lemma that he had previously overlooked, and that on several folios an entire column was crossed out. Obviously, therefore, it would not be feasible, as I had hoped, to publish the concordance in photographic facsimile.

Attempts to find a purchaser of the manuscript were not encouraging. Neither the British and Foreign Bible Society nor the American Bible Society showed any interest in using their funds, given for the publication of Bibles, to acquire the concordance. I wrote to my friend W. D. McHardy, the Regius Professor of Hebrew at Oxford, who had taken his D.Phil. degree in Syriac, and also to John Emerton, the Regius Professor of Hebrew at Cambridge, but apparently neither saw fit to get in touch with Mrs. Bonus.

During the 1960s I was invited several times to serve as external examiner of doctoral dissertations involving Syriac written under the supervision of Professor John Bowman, who by that time had moved from Leeds (see p. 165 below) to the University of Melbourne. It occurred to me that perhaps Bowman might be in a position to negotiate with Mrs. Bonus, and therefore I acquainted him with what I knew about the concordance. As it turned out, Dudley Hallam, a colleague in Bowman's department, was on a study leave in England, and arrangements were made for him to visit Mrs. Bonus. The outcome of that visit was the acquisition of the concordance by the Department of Middle Eastern Studies, University of Melbourne, for two hundred and fifty pounds sterling.[7]

Delegate to the ACLS

The letters ACLS stand for the American Council of Learned Societies, the origin of which was as follows. At

---

[7]Through the expertise of George A. Kiraz, there is now available *A Computer Generated Concordance to the Syriac New Testament* (6 vols.; Leiden: E. J. Brill, 1993).

the international conference of learned societies held at Paris in May 1919, which resulted in the formation of the Union académique internationale, the United States was represented by two of its existing societies, the American Academy of Arts and Sciences and the American Historical Association, there being no national academy devoted to the humanities. In order to consider the formation of such a central national organization, a conference of learned societies comprising delegates from ten societies of the United States was held at Boston in September 1919. At this conference it was decided to establish a central body consisting of representatives of each society, to be known as the American Council of Learned Societies. A constitution was adopted for subsequent ratification, and the council was formally organized February 14, 1920, with eleven constituent societies. With headquarters in New York City, the newly created American Council of Learned Societies also became affiliated with the Union académique internationale.

During the following years other learned societies in the United States became members of the ACLS; one of these was the Society of Biblical Literature. Each society elects a representative, called a delegate, to the ACLS for a term of four years, with the possibility of reelection once during any period of continuous tenure.

It was my lot in the late fifties to be elected delegate to the ACLS from the Society of Biblical Literature, succeeding in that office Erwin R. Goodenough of Yale University. Among the subjects discussed at meetings that I attended, the one that attracted the widest interest was how to persuade the Congress of the United States to create a National Foundation of the Arts and Humanities.

In the development of a strategy to bring to the attention of lawmakers the need for such a foundation, the ACLS, along with the Council of Graduate Schools in the United States and the United Chapters of Phi Beta Kappa, prepared a "Report of the Commission on the Humanities." Published in 1964, this report—a book of 225 pages—was drafted by the chairman of the commission, Barnaby C. Keeney, at that time president of Brown University. The volume was made up chiefly of individual reports from twenty-four constituent learned societies.

As would be expected, there was a certain amount of repetition among these reports, all of them recommending that Congress establish a National Foundation of the Humanities. In the case, however, of the report of the committee of the Society of Biblical Literature—a report drafted by Herbert G. May, Samuel Sandmel, Frederick V. Winnett, and myself as chair—special attention was drawn to the need for experimentation in the teaching of the biblical languages, the reprinting of major reference tools and scientific journals then out of print, and the provision of travel grants to enable American scholars to participate more widely in international congresses held abroad.

Several months after submitting our report, in February of 1965, I received word from the Honorable Frank Thompson, Jr., the chairman of the Special Subcommittee on Labor in the U.S. House of Representatives, stating that "work had begun in drafting a bill that would provide the necessary recognition, encouragement, and subvention of both the humanities and the performing and visual arts."

Later that year, after the bill was passed by both houses of Congress, the several delegates and secretaries of the constituent learned societies, with other guests as well, were invited to be present in the Rose Garden at the White House when President Johnson signed the bill into law.

The appointed time for the signing, September 29th, turned out to be a pleasant autumn day. Following announcements and brief comments made by several Congressmen, the bill was duly signed. The guests then formed in a line and passed by the president, who handed each of us a fountain pen bearing the seal of the United States of America and the signature of Lyndon B. Johnson.

Thesaurus Linguae Graecae

In 1971 a graduate student in classics inquired of her supervisor, Professor Theodore F. Brunner of the University of California at Irvine, why the library contained a Latin thesaurus but not a Greek thesaurus. He explained that the project to compile a Latin thesaurus had been organized by several German academies in the 1890s and that the volumes so far published had arrived only as far as the letter "M." Furthermore, since ten times as much Greek literature had survived as Latin, "You will understand," Brunner concluded, "why there is no Greek thesaurus." "That explanation does not satisfy me," responded his student, Mrs. Marianne McDonald. "If I give you a million dollars, will you organize a team and begin compiling a thesaurus of the Greek language?"

When Brunner had sufficiently recovered his composure, he replied that he would accept her offer. (Mrs. McDonald's father, I understand, was the founder—or co-founder—of the Zenith Radio Corporation.) Following her initial gift in 1972, Mrs. McDonald later provided additional support to the project. Subsequently she became professor of classics and theater at the University of California, San Diego.

At the outset Brunner requested the president of the American Philological Association, Professor William H. Willis of Duke University, to appoint an advisory committee to assist in planning the scope of the project. I was among the half-dozen scholars Willis appointed, with Douglas C. C. Young, professor of Greek, University of North Carolina at Chapel Hill, as convener.

We met in late February of 1973 at the Center for Hellenistic Studies at Washington, D.C. After considerable discussion we endorsed the decision that, instead of creating a traditional type of thesaurus, that is, a comprehensive lexicon citing and defining all (or essentially all) extant words in Greek within a specific chronological framework, Brunner's team would do well to make use of twentieth-century technology in order to create for the computer a data base of ancient Greek texts. It was decided that, when completed, the data base should reflect all ancient authors and texts extant from the period between Homer and AD 600.

At subsequent meetings convened at the University of California, Irvine, at Washington, at Urbana (where one of the committee members, the versatile Miroslav Marcovich, resided), and other places, we mainly discussed which edition of this or that ancient Greek author should be selected for data entry. Editions were selected on the basis of a number of considerations, including scholarly superiority of one text over other editions but also the relative recency and availability of the texts. Sometimes it was not possible to find a text that had gained the approval of all scholars. For example, there was some dissatisfaction with Migne's *Patrologia Graeca,* yet, for many authors, this was (and still is) the only printed text available. The least unsatisfactory solution seemed to be the recommendation that Migne be used for authors not otherwise in print, but that as more accurate editions emerged, the Migne text should be supplanted in the data bank.

After decisions had been made concerning editions, the material was sent to typists, who "read" the text into computers. On the basis of a test conducted among typists in Greece, Taiwan, and South Korea, it was discovered that the Koreans, though they had learned only the Greek alphabet, were able to maintain a higher degree of accuracy than typists in Greece.

Following the death of Professor Young in the autumn of 1973, Lionel Pearson, professor emeritus at Stanford University, served as convener of the committee until 1980. By early 1977, the project had gained sufficiently firm control over the period from Homer to AD 200 to complete data entry of the materials falling within this span. Approximately twenty million words then resided in the data bank, and the number of authors had grown to 2,884.

The original cutoff date of AD 600 for the thesaurus did not lend itself to either reality or realization. Many authors who antedate that date are recoverable only by consulting texts of later writers who quote them. In early 1985, therefore, as the thesaurus moved closer to the literature of Byzantium, Professor Ihor Ševčenko of Harvard University was appointed as chair, and the data base continued to expand. Subsequently, following a conference co-sponsored by the University of Athens Department of Linguistics and the Greek Ministries of Culture and Transportation, it was decided to extend the chronological limits of the thesaurus to the end of the Byzantine period in 1453. As of September 1996, Brunner was able to report statistics of its status as follows:

Corrected Text:	72,500,000 words
Uncorrected Text:	2,200,000 words
Total:	74,700,000 words

A letter from Brunner (dated February 6, 1996) explains that the Thesaurus Linguae Graecae data bank "includes all text materials surviving from the period between Homer and AD 600 plus scholia, lexicography, and historiography deriving from the 600–1453 period." In addition to the production of a CD-ROM, a spin-off of the project has been the publication of a volume, edited by Luci Berkowitz and Karl A. Squitier, entitled *Thesaurus Linguae Graecae: Canon of Greek Authors and Works.*[8]

Collected Works of Erasmus

Another project in which I was invited to participate was the production of an accurate, readable English translation of Erasmus's principal writings. This project was begun in 1969 by the University of Toronto Press and is expected to be completed early in the twenty-first century with eighty-six volumes containing the "Collected Works

---

[8]The third edition of this was issued by Oxford University Press, New York, in 1990.

of Erasmus." I was invited to be the general editor of the twenty volumes devoted to the New Testament scholarship of Erasmus (vols. 41–60). Because of my involvement in several other projects, I could not see my way clear to accepting another responsibility of such magnitude, and so I suggested that the Press approach Professor Robert D. Sider of Dickinson College, a careful and learned scholar in classics. Happily for all concerned, Sider accepted the appointment, and my own involvement has been limited to membership on the advisory committee of the entire project, as well as membership on the New Testament scholarship committee.

In order to bring the undertaking to the attention of a wider public audience, in the spring of 1984 the University of Toronto Press sponsored a series of four public lectures entitled The New Testament Scholarship of Erasmus. The series began with my lecture, "Vernacular Translations of the Scriptures Prior to Erasmus," and Sider concluded the series with a discussion, "The Definition of Biblical Language in the New Testament Scholarship of Erasmus."

·✑· Chapter 14 ·✑·

SABBATICAL LEAVES FROM TEACHING

U NTIL the early 1950s Princeton Theological Seminary had no policy of granting sabbatical leaves to the teaching staff. When such a program was instituted, the schedule involved granting one semester's leave every fifth year of teaching. My first such leave came during the academic year of 1958–59.

Early in July of 1958 I received a letter from Professor John Bowman of the University of Leeds, who stated that the university was inaugurating a six–month visiting lectureship to be called "The Montague Burton Lectureship" and invited me to be the first incumbent. As it happened, however, at that time I was suffering from a peptic ulcer that limited my normal activities. For this reason I thought it wise to decline Bowman's invitation, which was subsequently accepted by Professor Theodor Gaster of Columbia University. Despite my infirmity, however, I was able to continue working part-time on a book on textual criticism. This was published in 1964 under the title *The Text of the New Testament.* Four years later a German translation of the book was issued by the Kohlhammer Verlag of Stuttgart, and other translations have been published in Chinese, Italian, Japanese, Korean, and Russian.

Two of my most pleasant and productive sabbaticals were spent as a member of the school of historical studies at the Institute for Advanced Study in Princeton. Founded in 1930 through the benefactions of Louis Bamberger, a merchant and philanthropist, and of his sister, Mrs. Felix

Fuld, the institute was launched by the appointment of Abraham Flexner as director. Flexner had published several noteworthy analyses of higher education, of which his book entitled *Universities: American, English, and German*[1] was a widely praised study of European and American higher education. The first appointments of professors were made in 1932, Albert Einstein and Oswald Veblen, in the school of mathematics. Subsequently, three other schools were established: the school of historical studies in 1948, the school of natural sciences in 1966, and the school of social science in 1973. Each school has a small permanent faculty, the members of which devote themselves entirely to research. A total of some 160 fellowships at the institute are awarded annually to visiting members from other research institutions and universities throughout the world. Both the faculty and the annual members are given offices, secretarial assistance, and complete leisure in which to pursue their research.

My first association with the institute was during a sabbatical in the first semester of 1964–65. It goes without saying that I appreciated the opportunity to make contact with scholars from a wide spectrum of other disciplines. One such visiting scholar was the versatile and learned Günther Zuntz,[2] who at that time was working on a monograph published later under the title *Persephone*.[3] Among the permanent faculty members with whom I often had opportunity for conversation at the lunch table were Harold Cherniss (a specialist in Aristotle), Marshall Clagett (a specialist in ancient and medieval science), Otto Neugebauer (a polymath), Homer Thompson (an archaeologist), and Kenneth Setton (a medievalist).

It was during this sabbatical that I began preparing a text-critical commentary on the Greek New Testament.

---

[1]New York: Oxford University Press, 1930.

[2]The remarkable extent and depth of Zuntz's scholarship is detailed in Martin Hengel's obituary memoir of him published in the *Proceedings of the British Academy* 87 (1994) 493–522.

[3]Oxford: Clarendon, 1971.

This volume was designed to be a companion to the edition of the Greek New Testament soon to be published by the United Bible Societies (see pp. 71 and 73 n. 3 above). In it the reader learns something concerning the discussions of the committee in deciding which variant reading was to be placed in the text and which others in the apparatus.

The writing of the commentary, which entailed a consideration of more than two thousand sets of variant readings, proved to be a task far greater and much more exacting than it had appeared when I accepted Dr. Eugene Nida's invitation to produce such a volume. Every so often it would happen, in the process of evaluating the weight of manuscript evidence, that some question—whether great or small—would present itself as demanding resolution before I felt able to finish the report of the committee's discussion.

One such problem, for example, involved the presence or absence of the long ending of the Gospel of Mark (16:9–20) in Ethiopic manuscripts. Previously published statements by generally careful and reliable scholars were inadequate, confused, and contradictory. The same manuscripts were cited as containing or as not containing these verses, with or without a shorter ending standing between verses 8 and 9.

In order to begin to ascertain more fully and more accurately the evidence of Ethiopic witnesses, I combed through published catalogues of Ethiopic manuscripts located in libraries and museums of Europe and America and also wrote to curators of uncatalogued collections inquiring about the availability of Ethiopic manuscripts containing the Gospel according to Mark. In a few cases it was possible to examine the manuscripts themselves; in most cases arrangements were made to obtain photographic reproductions of those folios that, according to information given in the catalogues, contained the close of Mark's gospel.

Eventually I was able to gather evidence from sixty-five Ethiopic manuscripts, belonging to about thirty different collections. For all of them (except three), photographs, photostats, or microfilms of the ending of Mark's gospel are now on deposit in Princeton Seminary library. Following several months of research I was able to learn that in eighteen of the sixty-five Ethiopic manuscripts (including the three oldest manuscripts) the text of Mark 16:9–20 follows directly after verse 8. All of the remaining forty-seven manuscripts contain the shorter ending, which stands immediately following 16:8 and preceding verses 9–20.

Fortunately, not all of the problems that confronted me in writing the textual commentary entailed such extensive research. Nevertheless, it proved necessary following my sabbatical to continue to give attention to a great number of troublesome questions, and the commentary was still not finished by the time that my next sabbatical began in the spring of 1969. This time I spent the sabbatical with my wife at Tyndale House, Cambridge, where I was scholar in residence during the Easter term. The warden of Tyndale House, Derek Kidner, made accommodations available to us and gave me free use of the wonderful resources of the library. I was informed that the library's annual budget for books dealing with the Bible exceeded the budget of books in all areas of theology in the library of the Divinity School of the university. Finally the commentary was completed and published in 1971 by the United Bible Societies under the title *A Textual Commentary on the Greek New Testament.*

During my next sabbatical, in the spring term of 1974, I was back again as a member of the Institute for Advanced Study. This year the school of historical studies had begun a monthly colloquium at which papers were presented for discussion. I was invited to offer a paper and decided to discuss the controversial text known as the Nazareth Inscription. This is a Greek inscription that has been interpreted as reflecting official Roman reaction to a Jewish interpretation of the resurrection of Jesus Christ, namely, that the disciples had broken into the tomb and carried off the body (Matthew 28:12–15). As would be expected, the paper (which was published later in my book *New Testament Studies*)[4] aroused considerable discussion at the colloquium.

It was during this sabbatical that my attention was focussed on the ancient versions of the New Testament. Ever since the fifties, when I served as chair of the American Committee on Versions for the International Greek New Testament Project, I had been collecting information not only on the major early versions (Latin, Syriac, and Coptic) but also on the minor versions (Gothic, Armenian, Georgian, Ethiopic, Arabic, Nubian, and Sogdian), including even the Old Church Slavonic and the Anglo-Saxon, neither of which can really be termed an ancient version.

In seeking further information concerning several of these versions, I was able during the same sabbatical to spend some time at Cambridge University, where I was visiting fellow of Clare Hall, located conveniently near the university library. My wife and I enjoyed the coming of springtime and the glorious panorama of daffodils along the "backs" of colleges. At last I was able to consolidate my research into a rather substantial volume entitled *The Early Versions of the New Testament: Their Origin, Transmission, and Limitations*.[5] "Limitations" in the subtitle refers to the inability of the language of a given version to represent certain features of the Greek text. For example, Latin has no definite article; Syriac has no subjunctive or optative mood; Coptic has no passive voice. For the technical discussion of such matters I was able to secure the expertise of specialists who provided several signed contributions.

My last sabbatical prior to retirement from teaching was spent as visiting fellow at Wolfson College, Oxford. Here, during the spring term of 1979, my wife and I were able to compare living in Oxford with our earlier experience of living in Cambridge. We concluded that the ambiance of

---

[4] *New Testament Studies: Philological, Versional, and Patristic* (Leiden: E. J. Brill, 1980) 75–92.

[5] Oxford: Clarendon, 1977.

the two university cities is noticeably different and various features of each are superior to those of the other.

Two projects engaged my attention during this sabbatical. One involved the assembling of photographs and the writing of descriptions of forty-five manuscripts of the Greek Bible, each of which was of palaeographical and/or text-critical importance. These covered seventeen centuries and were arranged in chronological sequence. To these I prefixed a general discussion concerning the making of ancient books, the work of scribes in copying manuscripts, and the special features of biblical manuscripts that contain various "helps for readers." The book was published under the title *Manuscripts of the Greek Bible: An Introduction to Greek Palaeography*.[6] Several years later a Japanese translation of the volume appeared.

The other project was the development of a long-term interest of mine concerning the canon of the New Testament. Over the years I had, of course, touched upon this subject in teaching the required course, New Testament Introduction, but in time I developed a graduate seminar on the subject as well. Here it was possible to discuss in detail various Greek and Latin texts from the church fathers that have a bearing on the history of the growing recognition of the canon.

During the months of my sabbatical there was opportunity to present my ideas on the canon before various groups and to receive comments and criticisms. I was invited to give lectures at the Universities of Durham, St. Andrews, Glasgow, Edinburgh, Stirling, and Exeter, as well as to the Tyndale Fellowship and to the Divinity School in Cambridge. At most of these places I discussed the development of the canon and raised questions such as whether the canon is open or closed, how far one should look for a canon within the canon, and, still more basically, whether the canon is an authoritative collection of books or a collection of authoritative books.

---

[6]New York: Oxford University Press, 1981.

And so, after a long period of gestation, a volume was finally published that completed a trilogy of books on the text, the early versions, and the canon; it has the title *The Canon of the New Testament: Its Origin, Development, and Significance.*[7] A few years later a German translation was issued by the Patmos Verlag of Düsseldorf, and a Korean translation has also appeared; an Italian translation and a Russian translation are currently in preparation.

---

[7]Oxford: Clarendon, 1987.

·ᴏ· Chapter 15 ·ᴏ·

THE OXFORD COMPANION TO THE BIBLE

THE first of the Oxford Companions appeared in 1933; it was Sir Paul Harvey's *Oxford Companion to English Literature*.[1] The format has proved to be popular for similar volumes on a wide variety of other subjects. These include volumes on American history, American literature, Canadian history and literature, children's literature, classical literature, French literature, German literature, Italian literature, the literature of Wales, twentieth-century poetry, and women's writings in the United States. Other Oxford Companions deal with architecture, art, the English language, law, local and family history, music, philosophy, popular music, the theatre, twentieth-century art, world politics, and World War II. Still other Companions treat such topics as animal behavior, California, chess, Christian art and architecture, film, gardens, medicine, the mind, ships and the sea, sports and games, the Supreme Court, wine, and yachting. It was surprising to me that a Companion to the Bible had not been commissioned earlier in the sequence of these volumes. I learned later, however, that I was the third person whom Oxford approached as possible editor; apparently neither of the other two could reach a satisfactory understanding with the Press as to the nature and scope of the intended volume.

---

[1]Oxford: Clarendon. This volume is now in a revised edition, edited by Margaret Drabble, New York: Oxford University Press, 1990.

In 1983 David Attwooll, who had come from Britain to the New York office of Oxford University Press, wrote me suggesting that we explore the possibility of my editing *The Oxford Companion to the Bible*. After some preliminary discussion concerning the nature and scope of the volume, on the last day of July, 1984, the contract was signed. This specified that by the last of May, 1989, the completed manuscript of the book was to be delivered to the New York office of the Press.

It was perhaps unwise of me to agree to this date, for I had noticed in the preface of a dozen or more earlier Companions how often the editor mentioned that it had taken a decade or more to produce the volume. Since, however, I had just that year reached the mandatory retirement age at the Seminary (seventy years), I thought that, being relieved of teaching responsibilities, I would be able to meet the five-year stipulation.

The Oxford Companion to the Bible belongs, of course, to the category of dictionaries of the Bible, the production of which has had a long and varied history. What appears to be the first such work was produced about the year 330, when Eusebius of Caesarea compiled in alphabetical order a gazetteer of all the principal place-names occurring in the Bible, together with the corresponding Greek or current names, and succinct indications of relative location. This onomasticon was translated into Latin by Jerome, who provided some corrections and issued it in two parts, a *Book of Interpretation of Hebrew Names* and a *Book Concerning the Location and Names of Hebrew Places*.

Still more comprehensive was the work of Epiphanius of Salamis, who in 392 produced a biblical encyclopedia of the books and versions of the Old and New Testaments, the weights and measures occurring in the Bible, and the geography of places mentioned in the Bible. Since these early beginnings, many Bible dictionaries have been produced in many languages; those written in English now number considerably more than one hundred, many of which are cited in William M. Smith's bibliography of such volumes.

The first step was to draw up a list of categories of articles and of topics within each category. The lists were examined by editors of the Press at both Oxford and New York, and several modifications and additions were submitted for my consideration.

After further correspondence it was agreed that the volume should embrace the following broad categories of articles. Bearing on the formation of the Bible are articles on all the books of the Bible, as well as on the Apocrypha and the Pseudepigrapha. Inasmuch as the Bible has been continuously translated, reproduced, and disseminated, there needed to be entries on ancient writing, manuscripts, and book-making; on chapter and verse divisions; on the history and processes of printing and publishing the Bible; on illustrated, children's, and "curious" Bibles; on ancient, medieval, and modern translations of the Bible into all major language groups; and on the work of Bible societies in this regard.

Within the category of the biblical world are articles bearing on key individuals, events, dates, institutions, and realia of daily life in ancient Israel and the earliest Christian communities. Among biblical concepts and theological topics are biblical theology as such, as well as biblical views of such perennial issues as afterlife and immortality, creation, death, faith, hope, love, monotheism, and Satan. In the area of the interpretation of the Bible are separate treatments of the history, theory, and practice of interpretation, quotations from the Hebrew Bible in the New Testament, typology, fundamentalism, and anti-Semitism.

In addition to articles on all these topics, it was my idea to include a substantial number of articles dealing with the pervasive influence that the Bible has had on society, the arts, and Western culture in general. Particularly noteworthy has been the immense influence of the Scriptures on British, North American, European, and other literatures. It was decided therefore, that there should be a composite entry on literature and the Bible. In addition, about twenty other entries, identified by the phrase "———— and the Bible," were developed on such topics as African American traditions and the Bible, art and the Bible, dance and the Bible, Eastern Orthodoxy and the Bible, feminism and the Bible, Freud and the Bible, Jung and the Bible, Karl Marx and the Bible, law and the Bible, medicine and the Bible, Mormonism and the Bible, music and the Bible, politics and the Bible, popular culture and the Bible, the Qur'an and the Bible, and science and the Bible.

Along with identifying the scope of the various articles, decisions also had to be made concerning who should be invited to write the individual articles. An attempt was made, of course, to seek scholars who had already published definitive works on the subject matter. For example, since Claus Westermann of Heidelberg had written some three thousand pages of commentary on the book of Genesis, it was natural that he should be invited to prepare the article on that book. In light of the space available I could allow him three thousand words—an assignment that, happily, he accepted.

Inasmuch as during the preceding years invitations for lecture tours had taken me to Great Britain, Australia, New Zealand, and South Africa, I was able to consider a broad representation of international scholarship for contributions to the volume. A total of nearly two hundred scholars from twenty different countries responded to my letters of invitation.

Early in the solicitation of articles I committed an embarrassing blunder; I unwittingly invited two persons to write essentially the same article ("Day of Judgment" and "Judgment Day"). My mistake did not come to my attention until I received the two articles during the same week. What was to be done? Fortunately, my friend Paul Minear of Yale, who began his article on "Day of Judgment" by discussing the Old Testament expression "Day of the Lord," agreed to re-work his article somewhat so that it could be placed under the entry "Day of the Lord."

Among the dozen articles I chose to write myself, two were condensations of much longer articles that I had previously contributed to Festschriften in honor of Johannes Quasten and A. F. J. Klijn. The article entitled "Names for the Nameless" traces the growth of Jewish and Christian traditions that supplied names for persons who are mentioned in the Bible without an identifying name—such as Cain's wife, Noah's wife, Jephthah's daughter, the wise men at the birth of Jesus, the seventy disciples, the two criminals crucified with Jesus, and the Roman soldier who pierced Jesus' side. The other article, "Sortes Biblicae," discusses the use of the Scriptures in order to tell one's fortune, particularly by consulting specially prepared Greek and Latin copies of the Gospels furnished with annotations in the margins of successive pages.

The five years allocated for the completion of my work as compiler of the volume went by quickly, and I was a few months late in turning over to the Press the complete manuscript. Consequently, the New York office of the Press felt justified in inviting another editor to provide assistance in bringing the volume more speedily to completion. This was Michael D. Coogan, professor of religious studies at Stonehill College, North Easton, Massachusetts. Since Coogan was a Roman Catholic scholar trained in Old Testament studies, he provided an editorial balance that may have enhanced the appeal of the volume to the general public. Besides writing a number of articles himself, Coogan made suggestions for additional articles by former students of his that rounded out the coverage of the volume.

There was a sifting of articles by editors of the Press on both sides of the Atlantic. R. A. Denniston in the British office did not consider my proposed article on "Postage Stamps and the Bible" to be altogether suitable for inclusion in *The Companion* (see pp. 179–80 below), and the New York office decided that a dozen articles that I had solicited "did not fit comfortably in the scope of the volume." These latter were returned to the authors, who had been paid for writing them and who were given permission to use them elsewhere. Of course I wrote to the authors involved to say that I had nothing to do with the decision made by the editors at the Press. Happily, almost all of these authors had also written other articles which are included in the volume, and so their names still appear in the directory of contributors.

After the seven hundred or so articles had been set up in page proof, the Press employed two persons to draw up a detailed index of the contents of the articles. Such an index, which is altogether unusual in Bible dictionaries, makes *The Companion* a much more accessible reference tool.

In the United States *The Oxford Companion to the Bible* was published in October of 1993. In the weeks that followed publication, the New York office of the Press arranged for me to be interviewed by magazine editors, newspaper reporters, and radio talk-show hosts. Many of these were by telephone, but some were face-to-face. In October I participated in the Milton Rosenberg talk show in the studios of WGN Chicago. In November Coogan and I, while attending the annual meeting of the Society of Biblical Literature held that year in Washington, D.C., were interviewed by Bob Edwards on National Public Radio.

In Great Britain it was decided to publish *The Companion* in the spring of 1994. Nigel Lynn, manager of Bibles and liturgical books of the Oxford University Press, arranged for me to spend the week of Palm Sunday in England in order to make presentations in London, Oxford, and Cambridge in behalf of *The Companion.* An evening lecture about compiling a Bible dictionary, held at Dillon's Bookshop on Margaret Street in London, was followed the next day by broadcasts over local stations in various sections of Britain as well as on the World Service of the BBC. At Mansfield College, Oxford, I met one morning with members of the Faculty of Divinity, and in the evening spoke to students and others at an open meeting held in the old library of the Church of St. Mary the Virgin. Fliers announced that refreshments would be served and that signed copied would be available.

The day before Palm Sunday the chauffeur employed by the Press drove me to Gonville Hotel in Cambridge, for I was to deliver the sermon the next day in Great St. Mary's, the university church. I was identified among the notices in the church bulletin as co-editor of *The Oxford Companion to the Bible,* but other than this, nothing further was mentioned about the publication.

The actual launching of *The Companion* took place the following Tuesday evening (29 March) at a party held in the Jerusalem Chamber of Westminster Abbey. The guest list of about forty names was headed by Lord Donald Coggan, former archbishop of Canterbury (whom I had invited to write the article on the Lord's Prayer for *The Companion*), and James Arnold Baker, secretary to the delegates of the Oxford University Press. Unhappily the latter was unable to attend, since a day or two before the launching he had returned ill from a trip to Japan. In his place was Ivon Asquith, managing director of arts and reference books. After Coggan, Asquith, and I had each made some remarks about the new publication, a catering service provided refreshments and there was opportunity for conversation with the guests, many of whom were long-time friends of mine on the faculties at Oxford, Cambridge, King's College (London), and other British institutions.

The stately room in which we were meeting adjoins the southwest tower of the Abbey and gained its name, it is thought, from tapestries hung there that depicted matters pertaining to Jerusalem. The chamber is the traditional place of the death of King Henry IV and is referred to in this connection by Shakespeare at the close of Act IV of Part Two of his play by that name. This room had also been the venue for meetings of the London company of translators who produced the Authorized Version of 1611, its revisers of 1881–85, and the joint committee of churches that produced the New English Bible of 1970.

At the close of my visit of six days in Britain, during which there were some twenty interviews and other presentations concerning the making of *The Oxford Companion to the Bible,* I returned to Princeton, exhausted but with a certain feeling of satisfaction that, among the variety of Oxford Companions, there was at last one on the Bible.[2]

Addendum

What follows is the text of my brief article on "Postage Stamps and the Bible," originally intended for *The Oxford Companion to the Bible* (see p. 176 above).

Postage Stamps and the Bible. More than one thousand postage stamps, issued by thirty-some countries throughout the world, have, in one way or another, a link with the Bible. Some depict persons, plants, birds, and animals mentioned in the Scriptures; others commemorate noteworthy translations and editions of the Bible or include quotations from the Old or New Testament. In some cases stamps depict reproductions of biblical subjects from religious paintings, mosaics, stained-glass windows, tapestries, and illuminated manuscripts. The theme of the Holy Family or the Madonna and Child is most frequently portrayed, particularly for the Christmas season.

Stamps that have quotations from the Bible include the following: "Love thy neighbor as thyself" (Leviticus 19:18), issued by Israel in 1958 (Scott's *Standard Postage Stamp Catalogue* [No. 149; New York: Scott, 1990]); "In the beginning was the Word, and the Word was with God" (John 1:1), Czechoslovakia, 1975 (*Scott,* 209–11); "The greatest of these is charity" (1 Corinthians 13:13), New South Wales, 1897 (*Scott,* B1); "Peace among men of good will" (Luke 2:14), Switzerland, 1945 (*Scott,* 293–98); "They shall beat their swords into ploughshares" (Isaiah 2:4), the United Nations, 1967 (issued in six languages; *Scott,* 177–83).

---

[2]In 1996 a Polish translation of the volume was issued in Warsaw under the title *Słownik wiedzy biblijnej* (Warszawa: Oficyna Wydawnicza "Vocatio," 1996).

Stamps that commemorate translations and editions of the Bible include the following. In 1952 the United States of America issued a three-cent stamp (*Scott,* 1014) depicting Johannes Gutenberg showing to the Elector of Mainz a proof of a page of the first Bible printed with moveable type. In 1941 Sweden issued three stamps (*Scott,* 316–18) that commemorate the first complete Bible published in Swedish (the Gustav Vasa Bible of 1541). A Hungarian stamp issued in 1939 (*Scott,* B104) commemorates Gaspar Karoli, the translator of the entire Bible into Magyar, published in 1590. A stamp issued by Finland in 1948 (*Scott,* 277) depicts Mikael Agricola with his newly translated Finnish Bible, published in 1548.

In 1988, in response to a proposal made by the National Bible Society of Scotland and the Scottish Churches' Council, the British Post Office produced an aerogramme (26 pence) to coincide with the "Year of the Bible 1988" in Scotland, a celebration intended (as is stated on the aerogramme) "To increase popular awareness of the Bible as a relevant book for today." The exterior of the aerogramme commemorates, with pictures and quotations, six versions of the Scriptures.

BIBLIOGRAPHY: Baron, Gerhard. "Botschaft im Kleinformat; Bibelübersetzer auf Briefmarken." *Bibel Report* 4 (1980) 4ff.; Gould, A. E. *Postage Stamps and the Bible Story* (Valley Forge: Judson, 1968); Kibble, Daryl R. *The Old Testament Philatelic Catalogue* (Booval, Queensland, Australia: published in three parts by the compiler, 1988–89) [a superb reference work, with a checklist of biblical quotations and major subjects]; McCarthy, David S. *Devotions from a Stamp Album* (Grand Rapids, Mich.: Baker, 1983); Matek, Ord. *The Bible through Stamps* (New York: Ktav, 1974); Mueller, Barbara. *Postage Stamps and Christianity* (St. Louis: Concordia, 1964); Sun, Thomas. *The Bible on Postage Stamps* (Taipei: Hua Ming, 1973); *Stamps, Famous Paintings and the Good News* (Hong Kong Bible Society, 1981) [in English and Chinese].

·❧· Chapter 16 ·❧·

ON THE LECTURE CIRCUIT
AT HOME AND ABROAD

O VER the years invitations came to me to present
lectures—whether one lecture or a series of lectures—at considerably more than one hundred colleges, seminaries, and universities. In the United States
these ranged alphabetically from Abilene Christian University to Yale University, and abroad from the University of
Aberdeen to the University of Zululand. In some cases I
was asked to return to the same institution several times, as,
for example, Asbury Theological Seminary, Brigham Young
University, Southwestern Baptist Theological Seminary, University of Georgia, Western Theological Seminary (Holland, Michigan), and Wheaton College (Illinois).

Several of the invitations were to present named lec-
ture series. In 1961 I gave the Adolf Olson Memorial Lectures at Bethel Theological Seminary, St. Paul, Minnesota.
These were later incorporated, much expanded and supple-
mented, in my book *The New Testament: Its Background,
Growth, and Content.* Other special lectures were the Henry
Barton Robinson Lecture in Religion at Culver-Stockton
College, Canton, Missouri, issued later in pamphlet form;
the Day-Higgenbotham Lectures at Southwestern Baptist
Theological Seminary, Fort Worth, as well as, in a sub-
sequent year, the Huber Drumwright Memorial Lectures at
the same institution; the Humanities Lecture at Boston
College; the First Colwell Lecture at Claremont School of
Theology; the D. A. Barber Lecture, Kingsville, Texas; the

Griffith Thomas Lectures at Dallas Seminary; the Walling Lectures, Abilene Christian University; and the Willson Lectures at Trinity University, San Antonio, Texas.

In other cases the invitation was to give a course of lectures that extended for several weeks or months. In 1970 I served as distinguished visiting professor at Fuller Theological Seminary, Pasadena; in 1978 as visiting professor at Gordon-Conwell Theological Seminary, South Hamilton, Massachusetts; in 1978 as lecturer at New College, Berkeley; in 1982 as visiting professor at North Park Theological Seminary, Chicago; and in 1994 as guest professor at the Reformed Theological Seminary, Orlando Campus, Florida.

Invitations came to me from a dozen different academic institutions that participated in the Staley Distinguished Christian Scholar Lecture Program. This program was a project of the Thomas F. Staley Foundation of New York, established in 1969 in order to provide funds so as "to bring to college and university campuses in America distinguished Christian scholars . . . for Spiritual Enrichment Weeks, special lecture series, and seminars on basic Christianity." The foundation is independent of any other institution, and cooperates with academic institutions that seek financial assistance in attracting lecturers to their campus. Such invitations have usually involved giving several lectures to the student body as a whole, participation in one or more classroom presentations correlated to the subject matter of the course, lunch or dinner with faculty members, and making oneself available for individual discussion with students.

In addition to many invitations to lecture at institutions in the United States, quite a number of invitations involved travel abroad. My first opportunity to give a series of lectures in another country came when I was invited to spend several weeks during 1952 at two Presbyterian seminaries in Brazil—a country that I learned is larger than the continental United States of America.

The larger and older of the two institutions was located at Campinas, about two hundred miles west of Rio de

Janeiro. The dean and librarian of the seminary, Waldyr Carvalho Luz, had received a few years earlier the Th.D. degree in New Testament from Princeton Seminary. His dissertation was on the subject, "The Apostle Paul in Contemporary Roman Catholic Thought."

The interpreter for my lectures was an American missionary, Rev. Philip S. Landes, a graduate of Princeton Seminary in 1910; he and his wife kindly invited me to stay in their home while I was in Campinas. My lectures at the seminary involved two series, one dealing with the exegesis of Paul's Letter to the Galatians, and the other on recent developments in New Testament research. During one of the five weeks of lecturing to the students I was also invited to give a series of lectures at the annual Pastors' Conference held at the seminary.

During weekends there were opportunities for sightseeing, and on one such weekend I went by bus to Rio de Janeiro. Here the chief tourist attraction was to go by cable car to the top of Sugar Loaf Mountain, from which one can see much of the sprawling city of Rio, as well as, in the distance, the colossal statue of Christ the Savior, with arms outstretched.

On another weekend I was taken by car to see some of the countryside. I was intrigued by jaboticaba trees with their sweet cherry-like fruit. The round, blue-black pulpy jaboticaba grows directly on the branches and even in rows down the trunk of the tree *(Myrciaria cauliflora)*. Remarkable for a totally different reason was a visit to a poisonous reptile farm. Here we saw an attendant in a white gown "milking" snakes of their venom, which was then used in toxicological research in order to produce serums useful in counteracting snakebites.

During the last ten days of my visit to Brazil I lectured at the Presbyterian Seminary at Recife, a seacoast city located eight degrees south of the equator. Even though it was September I found the heat and humidity of this place most oppressive. The president of the seminary, the Reverend Samuel Falcâo, had arranged for me to give two lectures a day, one in the late afternoon addressed primarily to students, and the other in the evening for laity and pastors who had come for a conference at the nearby Church of Boa Vista.

There was also opportunity during the week to make a visit and to speak at a small Congregational seminary nearby. As was true also at Campinas, I found students and pastors alike quite willing to listen to lectures even though they were conveyed through an interpreter, one sentence at a time.

In 1958 I participated in the Eleventh International Congress of Byzantinists, held at Munich. Here I presented a paper entitled "When Did Scribes Begin to Use Writing Desks?" Strange though it may seem, there appears to be no evidence—artistic, literary, or archaeological—prior to the seventh Christian century that scribes used a table or desk for writing.[1] Scribes ordinarily sat and held the writing material on their knees. (I am now able to add the support of G. M. Parássoglou, "A Roll upon His Knees," *Yale Classical Studies* 28 [1985] 273–75.)

On several occasions I was able to attend the Oxford Conference on Patristic Studies or the similar Oxford Conference on Biblical Studies. The first time, in 1955, I presented a short account concerning the International Greek New Testament Project during the session dealing with "Instrumenta Studiorum." In 1971 I read a paper on "The Practice of Textual Criticism among Church Fathers." Then, in 1973, Dr. H. F. D. Sparks invited me to deliver the main paper at one of the four evening sessions. I chose to deal with problems concerning the recognition of the canon of the New Testament. In 1975 I presented a short paper on the problematical Thracian version of the Gospels.

In the autumn of 1979 I was greatly surprised and highly pleased to receive a letter from Fr. Patrick Rogers,

---

[1] The so-called writing desks used by scribes at Qumran are only 17½ inches high and slightly concave lengthwise, much more suitable for use as a bench than a writing desk.

C.P., the secretary of the Irish Biblical Association, inviting me to present two lectures at the 1980 Spring Meeting of the association. Of course I accepted the invitation (which also included my wife as guest of the association) and proposed that at the two lectures I would deal with "Problems Old and New in Bible Translating" and "The Prayer That Jesus Taught His Disciples." Subsequent correspondence confirmed that these subjects would be suitable and also brought information concerning other parts of the program. The presidential address that year was to be delivered by Brian Nolan, who was lecturer in biblical studies and fundamental theology at All Hallows Missionary College, Dublin, and two lectures on the Epistle to the Ephesians were to be given by Ernest Best, a long-time friend of mine, then at St. Andrews, Scotland.

Father Rogers, it seems, had informed Professor F. E. Vokes, dean of the Faculty of Arts, Trinity College, Dublin, that I would be visiting Dublin. Consequently, Vokes, whom I had met some years before at an Oxford Patristic Congress, invited me to give a lecture at Trinity the day before the sessions of the Biblical Association were scheduled to begin.

The venue of the Biblical Association was the Bellinter Conference Centre, a lovely Georgian mansion on the main Dublin-Navan road, overlooking the river Boyne. Not only was the place of meeting delightful at the end of April, but the opportunity to meet several colleagues whom I had known previously, as well as to make new friends, was most gratifying.

The three days following the conference were the high point of our visit in Ireland. Father Rogers had earlier proposed to give us a tour of the Emerald Isle in his Fiat, and I agreed on the proviso that he would allow us to meet the expenses of such a trip. The first day we travelled through Yeats country, passed by Lough Gill, saw the Glencar Waterfall, and stayed overnight at Ballymote, County Sligo. The next day, after visiting Ballina, County Mayo, we went on to Achill Island, the westernmost part of Ireland, where

Father Rogers decided to take a swim in the Atlantic. We stayed overnight at Galway. On the third day we were taken through the scenic drive known as the Ring of Kerry, and thence to Killarney, Limerick, and back to All Hallows College once again.

On the following day my wife and I were entertained at lunch with the biblical lecturers at Milltown Institute of Dublin. In the afternoon Professor Martin McNamara, whose special interests included such disparate subjects as the Jewish Targums and Irish apocryphal writings, showed us through Maynooth Abbey, where we had our evening meal. Flying back the next day to the United States closed a memorable week of lecturing and sightseeing.

The next year found me once again on the other side of the Atlantic. The University of Cambridge Faculty of Divinity and the master and fellows of Emmanuel College had invited me to give a lecture in the old library of Emmanuel on the work of F. J. A. Hort as textual critic of the New Testament. The lecture, delivered on May 5, 1981, was to commemorate the centenary of the publication in 1881 of the Greek New Testament edited by Westcott and Hort. Volume 2, which contains Hort's magisterial introduction to the text-volume, provides a detailed account of the critical principles he and Westcott followed in preparing their celebrated edition of the Greek text.

The number of persons who attended the lecture at five o'clock was not large, but among them, I was told later, was a descendant of the scholar who was being honored. My lecture, which was entitled "The Westcott and Hort Greek New Testament—Yesterday and Today," was published later that year.[2]

Some weeks after returning to Princeton I received a letter from the librarian of Emmanuel College informing me that he had come upon an extra copy of Dr. Hort's picture and asking whether I would like to have it. Of course I wrote back immediately saying how pleased I

---

[2] *The Cambridge Review* (20 November 1981) 71–76.

would be to receive it. When it arrived I was still more delighted to see that it was a portrait-like picture, about 10 by 12 inches in size. It now hangs in my seminary office.

On the days following the Cambridge lecture, I presented a lecture at both St. David's University College, Lampeter, Wales, and the Theological College of the Presbyterian Church of Wales, located at Aberystwyth on the west coast of Wales.

Inasmuch as the current Welsh Bible, dating from 1620, was soon to be issued in a long-awaited revision, I decided to discuss the kinds of problems that confront all Bible translators, irrespective of the language involved. Like Ireland earlier in the twentieth century, many areas of Wales were experiencing a quite considerable pressure to revive and strengthen the use of the native tongue as a rival to English. Following my lecture at Aberystwyth I went on a short sightseeing tour through striking Welsh countryside, travelling on the Reidol Vale, a narrow-gauge railway that terminated at a station named Devil's Bridge.

The following year (1984), and this time accompanied by my wife, I undertook a much longer journey—to the other side of the globe. Edwin A. Judge, professor of history at Macquarie University at North Ryde, New South Wales, had invited me to lecture at Macquarie, where I would be a visiting research fellow. At Judge's suggestion I drew up a list of a dozen subjects on which I was prepared to present lectures before various kinds of groups. On the basis of that list Judge arranged for visits to several other institutions in the eastern part of Australia as well as in New Zealand.

Macquarie University was a newly established university that had opened for students in 1967. Already a thriving, pulsating institution, by 1984 several projects in the sciences as well as the liberal arts were being formulated and developed. The English department of the young university had published a useful dictionary of Australian English. Judge, who studied classics at Cambridge, had joined others in the formation of the Ancient History Documentary Centre, of which he became director in 1981. Fundamental in supporting

Judge's interests was the library's acquisition of published editions of documentary Greek papyri as well as hitherto unedited Greek papyri.

Among the Greek papyri acquired by the university was a scrap of papyrus measuring four inches tall and one-half inch wide, containing on each side three or four letters in eleven successive lines. After patient investigation the text was identified in 1981 by Stuart R. Pickering, senior research assistant in papyrology, as Acts 2:30–37 and 2:46–3:2. Dated to the third century, this fragment is referred to in recent editions of the Greek New Testament as $\mathfrak{P}^{91}$.

A long-range project proposed in 1979 by the Reverend Bruce Winter, then a lecturer at Moore Theological College but later the head of the School of History, Philosophy, and Politics at Macquarie, was to use the documentary resources of the university for the revision of Moulton and Milligan's *Vocabulary of the Greek Testament, Illustrated from the Papyri and Other Non-Literary Sources.*[3]

As a step toward the revision of Moulton and Milligan, Greg H. R. Horsley was appointed research assistant under a Macquarie University research grant. His task was to make a systematic search year-by-year through publications of Greek papyri and inscriptions searching for philological and historical information bearing on early Christianity. Horsley's analysis of Greek inscriptions and papyri published in 1976 was issued in 1981 under the title, *New Documents Illustrating Early Christianity.*[4] In succeeding years other volumes appeared, each providing a valuable summary and discussion of relevant data that can be used in the revision of Moulton and Milligan's *Vocabulary.*

While I was visiting research lecturer at Macquarie, my wife and I were staying at Dunmore Lange College, North Ryde, which made it convenient to visit neighboring

---

[3]This was first published in fascicles from 1914 to 1929 (London: Hodder & Stoughton).

[4]North Ryde, N.S.W.: The Ancient History Documentary Research Centre, Macquarie University.

colleges. I was invited to lecture at Robert Menzies College, at Moore Theological College, Newtown, and at the Baptist Theological College of New South Wales, located at Eastwood.

Our stay at Macquarie happened to coincide with a two-day symposium, sponsored by the Ancient History Documentary Research Centre, on the subject, "The Graeco-Roman Cultural Setting of the Conflict between Paul and the Corinthians." After introductory remarks had been made by Judge, papers were read by a galaxy of Australian scholars, including B. W. Winter, P. Marshall, B. Thiering, C. Forbes, P. Watkins, J. Court, B. W. Powers, G. H. R. Horsley, J. Painter, and P. W. Barnett. In the concluding remarks, which I had been asked to make, I focussed on problems of methodology in the study of the relationship between early Christianity and the mystery religions, enlarging upon what I had written on this subject in the *Harvard Theological Review*.[5]

Following a busy and productive visit at Macquarie University, my next base of speaking engagements was Queensland University, St. Lucia, and at institutions in and near Brisbane. These included Trinity Theological College at Toowong and the Roman Catholic seminary at Banyo. At Trinity I made the acquaintance of a professor of Old Testament from Holland, Hendrik C. Spykerboer, whose interests included translation of the Bible into Australian aboriginal languages. In a subsequent year I invited him to write the article on this subject for *The Oxford Companion to the Bible*.

From Brisbane my wife and I flew south to Melbourne, where our hosts were Principal and Mrs. Morris Betteridge of Ridley College, part of the University of Melbourne. One of Betteridge's hobbies was bookbinding, at which he was quite expert. His equipment for this kind of work seemed to me to be extensive as well as professional.

---

[5]Volume 48 (1955) 1–20.

In addition to my presenting lectures to students at Ridley, Betteridge arranged for me to speak to the United Theological Faculty, comprising members from three institutions: Trinity, a high Anglican college, Ormand, the Uniting Church college, and the Jesuit college. Before the week was over I also presented two lectures on "Making Sense of the Book of Revelation" to alumni of Ridley who were meeting for a ministers' conference at their alma mater.

Among people in Melbourne with whom I had previous contact was Professor John Bowman, who several years before had proposed my name as external examiner of doctoral dissertations that involved the Syriac language. One of his recent graduates was Terry Falla, originally from Guernsey, one of the Channel Islands, and at that time the Baptist chaplain at La Trobe University. Falla was currently at work on an outgrowth of his dissertation, the compiling of an analytical concordance to the Peshitta Syriac Gospels, which later I accepted for publication in the series, New Testament Tools and Studies.

Along with Professor John Painter of the Department of Religious Studies at La Trobe, Falla arranged for me to speak to the Fellowship of Biblical Studies, an organization that met regularly for the presentation and discussion of papers. The topic they suggested for me was, "Rigorous and Reasoned Eclecticism in New Testament Textual Criticism."

Falla was responsible for arranging two other speaking engagements, one at La Trobe University and the other at an ecumenical community in Melbourne. The one at La Trobe constituted the final lecture in a series begun earlier that year by the chaplains and entitled "Jesus and the Gospels." The other lecture was part of a weekend of biblical studies held at the House of the Gentle Bunyip. "The Bunyip," as it was called in Melbourne, was a unique Christian community, which had had, I believe, a significant ministry in the inner city and made an important contribution to the churches of Victoria.

Following our weeks in Australia, my wife and I spent a week in New Zealand. Here we were intrigued by the flora and fauna typical of those islands. Professor Judge, himself a New Zealander, had arranged for us to stop off first at the College of St. John the Evangelist in Auckland. This divinity school had been founded in the middle of the previous century by the first Anglican bishop of New Zealand, George A. Selwyn, in whose memory Selwyn College, Cambridge, was founded in 1881. By wise foresight, Bishop Selwyn had acquired for the newly founded seminary an extensive area of land on which, as it turned out, a major part of the city of Auckland was to develop in the following years.

The warden of the college, the Reverend Raymond Petty, who had spent a short time studying at Harvard Divinity School, arranged for us to stay in the guest flat of the college and placed us in the charge of the Reverend Francis Foulkes, who was lecturer in New Testament. Besides asking me to present several lectures to the entire student body, Foulkes had me teach two of his exegetical classes. Arrangements were also made for me to lecture, and then have lunch with the faculty, at the New Zealand Baptist College, located at Remuera, a suburb of Auckland. Sunday morning and evening I preached at two Presbyterian churches in Auckland.

Before leaving Auckland for Dunedin on the southern island of New Zealand, we had the pleasure of having tea in the home of Dr. and Mrs. G. A. F. Knight in St. Heliers, another suburb of Auckland. Knight, an Old Testament scholar from St. Andrews, Scotland, and later at McCormick Theological Seminary in Chicago, was invited in 1968 become principal of the newly established Pacific Theological College in the University of the South Pacific, located at Suva in the Fiji Islands. Having retired to Auckland, he was still active, primarily in writing and editing volumes of a devotional commentary on the books of the Old Testament.

When we stepped off the plane in Dunedin (which is Gaelic for Edinburgh), we found a light snow on the ground—a sharp contrast to the beautiful flowers blooming in the Knights' garden and elsewhere in Auckland. We were met at the airport by Gavin Munro, lecturer in biblical studies in Knox College, which comprises the Faculty of Theology in the University of Otago. In accord with earlier correspondence, I presented a lecture at Knox on "Present-Day Trends in the Textual Criticism of the New Testament." Following the lecture I was happy to meet not only students and several members of the Faculty of Theology but also—and especially—Agathe Thornton of the Department of Classics at Otago University. Her books, *People and Themes in Homer's Odyssey* and *The Living Universe: Gods and Men in Virgil's Aeneid,* had been widely discussed and appreciated.[6]

Arrangements had also been made for me to lecture at Holy Cross College, a Roman Catholic seminary at Mosgiel, several miles from Dunedin. The preference expressed by the authorities at Holy Cross was for me to present a lecture on the Lord's Prayer.

Some days later the homeward journey provided opportunity for assessing the five weeks spent "down under." I had given thirty presentations at twenty different locations. Having made new friends and acquaintances, my wife and I agreed that we were bringing back many pleasant memories that would remain with us for a long time.

In 1985 my wife and I travelled once again to the southern hemisphere, this time to South Africa in response to an invitation to lecture at twelve of the sixteen universities in that country. The organization for the lecture tour was arranged by Professor J. C. Coetzee, dean of the Faculty of Theology at Potchefstroom University, and by Jacobus Petzer, a doctoral student in New Testament at Potchefstroom. Several years earlier Petzer had come to Princeton Seminary in order to study Greek palaeography with me in preparation for writing his dissertation in the area of textual criticism of the Greek New Testament.

Because my listing of subjects proposed for lectures to various kinds of groups had seemed to work well for the

---

[6]Dunedin: University of Otago Press in association with Methuen, 1970; Dunedin: University of Otago Press, 1976.

visit to Australia and New Zealand, I drew up a somewhat similar list for the South African visit, and Dean Coetzee prepared an itinerary that took ease of travel into account.

En route to South Africa we stopped off at Oslo, in order to attend the meeting of the international Society of New Testament Studies held that year at Trondheim. From London a week later we flew to Johannesburg and went immediately to Potchefstroom.

After two days of rest as guests of Potchefstroom University, I was ready to begin the sequence of lectures at various locations, starting at the University of Zululand (Natal). Travelling by air to Durban we were driven about eighty miles north to the main campus of the university. This campus, founded in 1960, is mainly a residential university with board and lodging facilities for about two thousand students. The gymnasium, we were told, is the third largest in the world without interior supports for the roof.

Besides the Faculty of Theology, which awards degrees of B.Th., B.Th. (Honours), M.Th., D.Th., and B.Th. (Arts), there are also faculties of arts, science, law, economic and political sciences, and education. The Institute for Public Service and Vocational Training offers in-service courses leading to qualification with a variety of diplomas, preparing students for the public and private sectors.

On arrival at the main campus we were welcomed for lunch at the home of Professor Nicole S. L. Fryer. Present also were the Reverend Empangeni Mngadi, lecturer in Old Testament, Mr. Ngcongwanin, who lectured in Bantu, as well as the dean, Dr. B. J. Odendaal. Following two days at the University of Zululand, we were driven to the University of Durban-Westville, where we were entertained at the home of Dr. and Mrs. Pieter J. Maartens. Over the weekend we visited the University of Natal in Pietermaritzburg, where Professor Victor Bredenkamp, who had a doctorate from Princeton University, was our host.

We returned by air to Johannesburg and were driven by car to several universities where Afrikaans was the prevailing medium of instruction, though English was also widely used. At Pretoria are located the University of South Africa and the University of Pretoria. The former university, commonly called Unisa, has been since 1946 a correspondence and examination institution, with about one hundred thousand students. My lectures were for the benefit of members of the theological staff. Among these I recall most vividly Izak J. Du Plessis and Johnnie H. Roberts, both in the area of New Testament, and Willem S. Vorster, director of the Institute for Theological Research.

The University of Pretoria has two theological faculties. The professor of New Testament for the Dutch Reformed Church was Andrie B. Du Toit, who had recently published an excellent book on the canon of the New Testament.[7] Du Toit's counterpart in the faculty for the Dutch Reformed Church of South Africa was A. G. van Aarde.

In Johannesburg I gave lectures at two universities. One was the University of Witwatersrand, where I addressed the alumni and made the acquaintance of Dr. Patrick J. Hartin of the Department of Divinity. Later in the week we spent several days at the Rand Afrikaans University, which had been founded in 1966. The professor of biblical studies was Paul J. Du Plessis.

The next three universities on our itinerary were chiefly Afrikaans in orientation. They were the University of the Orange Free State at Bloemfontein, Potchefstroom University for Christian Higher Education, and the University of Stellenbosch. At Stellenbosch University, which is often called the Harvard of South Africa, I was pleased to see once again Professor H. J. Bernard Combrink, whom I had met in previous years when he spent a sabbatical at the University of Pennsylvania and had visited Princeton Seminary.

At Cape Town, besides giving lectures at the university, I took the opportunity of examining two Greek New

---

[7] J. H. Roberts and A. B. Du Toit, *Guide to the New Testament* (3d ed.; trans. D. R. Briggs; Pretoria: NG Kerkbockhandel, 1989).

Testament manuscripts in the public library of that place (see pp. 155–56 above). The headquarters of the Bible Society of South Africa is located in Cape Town, and the secretary general of the society, Gerrit van der Merwe, kindly drove us on a sightseeing tour through part of the surrounding fruit- and wine-producing region. At the town of Paarl we stopped to view an unusual monument. This was a stone shaft about forty feet high, erected in commemoration of the Afrikaans language.

Afrikaans, one of the official languages of the Republic of South Africa, developed from the language of the Boers, the Dutch immigrants who arrived in the middle of the seventeenth century. The first attempts to reduce Afrikaans to writing were the result of a desire to produce a Bible in this language. As early as 1872 a Dutchman, Arnoldus Panneris, a teacher at Paarl, argued that the States General edition of the Dutch Bible was virtually a closed book to the Afrikaans-speaking population. Eventually several books of the Bible were translated into the dialect, and in 1933 the entire Bible was published at Cape Town, exactly fifty years after the entire Bible had been translated into Zulu.

The next day Dr. van der Merwe entertained my wife and me at luncheon in the Bible House, with two other guests, Dr. and Mrs. E. P. Groenewald. Groenewald, a former professor of New Testament at the University of Pretoria, had been chairman of the committee that issued a revision of the Afrikaans Bible in 1983. While at the luncheon table my wife commented to Mrs. Groenewald that the previous day we had been taken to see the monument to the Afrikaans language. At the mention of the monument Mrs. Groenewald broke out with a vehement expression of disapproval of the monument. It seems that ever since its erection several years earlier people had been divided on the appropriateness of having a monument to commemorate a living language.

After leaving Cape Town and going on to the University of Port Elizabeth, which is located in Cape Province, my wife and I were entertained by Professor and Mrs. J. Wentzel van Huyssteen. Van Huyssteen had recently been awarded two prestigious prizes following the publication of a book later translated into English under the title *Theology and the Justification of Faith*.[8] Subsequently he has become the James I. McCord Professor of Theology and Science at Princeton Theological Seminary.

The last of the South African universities we visited was the University of Rhodes, located at Grahamstown, about four hours from Port Elizabeth. We made the trip itself uneventfully by public transport in a small van called the Leopard Express. There must have been, however, some confusion in the scheduling of our journey, for when the Leopard Express arrived at its destination in Grahamstown, no one was waiting there to meet us. After standing on the sidewalk for half an hour, I decided to look for a public telephone. Fortunately I had been given the name of the person at whose home we were to stay—the only instance on our itinerary when this kind of information had been provided. As it turned out, the public telephone was not in working order and so I was unable to get in touch with our hosts, Professor and Mrs. John Suggit.

Across the street from the telephone kiosk was a large church building—it was, in fact, the Anglican cathedral of St. Michael and St. George. Going there to seek assistance, I explained our plight to the only person whom I found sitting in the sanctuary—who happened to be the bishop! He said that he knew Suggit and would drive my wife and me to our destination.

A half hour later we were ringing the doorbell of the Suggits' home. One can imagine our embarrassment when we learned that the Suggits were expecting us to arrive the following day. Mrs. Suggit assured us, however, that our room was ready for our occupancy. In view of our unexpected early arrival, we insisted that the Suggits be our guests for dinner that evening at a local hotel. The next

---

[8]Translated by H. F. Snijders; Grand Rapids, Mich.: Eerdmans, 1989.

evening Mrs. Suggit entertained us, along with several other guests, including the bishop and his wife, and Dr. Jean Branford, the editor of a dictionary of South African English.

Our stay in Grahamstown coincided with the observance of an act of civic penitence throughout South Africa. The previous month several hundred concerned Christian leaders of various denominations had met at Pietermaritzburg and called for a National Initiative for Reconciliation. A detailed call for action, known as the Kairos Document, was issued in pamphlet form entitled "Challenge to the Church: A Theological Comment on the Political Crisis in South Africa." It was decided that on October 9, 1985, Christians across the nation should join in observing a day of prayer, mourning, and fasting, so that "our land may repent of its sins, be healed, and enter a new day of justice and equality for all."

On the stated day, members of the Rhodes University staff and student body met at 9:30 A.M. for a service in the Rhodes chapel, and at 12:45 P.M. for intercessory prayers in the Great Hall. At 5:00 P.M. a united church service was held in Grahamstown City Hall. The hymns, the prayers of intercession, an act of penitence, the readings of holy Scripture (Micah 6:6–8; 2 Corinthians 5:14–19; Romans 12:17–21), and the call to reconciliation, all combined to make a moving and memorable service.

After my final lecture on the following day, my wife and I flew to Johannesburg, and from there to the United States. Despite earlier reports in newspapers of civil unrest in parts of South Africa, at no time during our weeks of travel in that country did we ourselves happen to witness any such disturbances.

In November of 1985 I was invited to participate in the Twenty-first Annual Conference on Editorial Problems, held at the University of Toronto and organized by Richard Landon, the librarian in charge of the university's rare book collection. At the conference Stanley Wells of Oxford read a paper on "Revision in Shakespeare's Plays," and Leonard Boyle, librarian of the Vatican collections, read a paper on

"The Place of Codicology in the Editing of Mediaeval Latin Texts." Four other papers were presented, including mine on "History of the Editing of the Greek New Testament." All six papers were subsequently published under the title *Editing and Editors: A Retrospect.*[9]

In 1986 my wife and I were once again making a lengthy journey. A former Th.M. student of mine, Chae-Woon Na, who had become a professor at the Presbyterian Theological Seminary in Seoul, South Korea, arranged with Dr. Chang-Whan Park, the president of the seminary, to invite me to teach an exegetical course for M.Div. students, as well as a course on methodology of New Testament studies for the students in the Graduate Program for Third-World Leaders. The latter group was extremely diversified. In addition to students from several Oriental countries, there were also students from countries in Africa, Indonesia, and the Philippines, and even two from the United States.

From time to time during our stay in Seoul we were driven about in that teeming city, in which one-fourth of the total population of South Korea resides. We were constantly amazed at the great number of churches, each of which could be identified at night by a red illuminated cross. We were told that about 23 percent of the population of Korea was Christian. Of this total, a large number belonged to several different Presbyterian denominations.

The largest Presbyterian congregation was the Young-Nak Church, with some forty thousand members, served by eighteen pastors, and with six services of worship every Sunday—each with a separate choir of some eighty members. On one of the Sundays it was my privilege to preach at the three morning services. Later during our stay in Korea the annual two-day conference of the Association of Professors of Theology was held at Kyongju, about 160 miles southeast of Seoul. We travelled there by train and I addressed the group both afternoons.

[9]New York: AMS, 1988.

Just before our departure from Korea at Kimpo Airport, a banquet in a Chinese restaurant was held in my honor, at which there were twenty Korean pastors who were alumni of Princeton Seminary. I was happy to renew my friendship with them, many of whom had been in my classes.

From Korea we flew to Japan, where we were met at Marita Airport by a former Th.M. student of mine, Takeshi Nagata, who drove us to the International Christian University. This university, founded in 1949, has had a steady growth, with more than two thousand students enrolled at the time of our visit in 1986. Ninety-one percent of these students were Japanese and the rest were from twenty-seven other countries. One of the professors, Carl Ferruya, had earned the Th.D. degree in theology from Princeton Seminary. Besides participating in the academic program of the university, Dr. Ferruya also served as the director of the Institute for the Study of Christianity and Culture.

The visit at the International Christian University was followed by further lectures at the Tokyo Union Theological Seminary. Happily it was also possible to visit the Japanese Bible Society, and to make the acquaintance of the general secretary, Motoaki Tanabe.

Although I had been invited to visit Doshisha University in Kyoto (said to be the most beautiful city in Japan), our schedule did not permit making this additional journey. Shigeo Hashimoto, the professor of New Testament at Doshisha and a former doctoral student of mine, was able to visit us in Tokyo. It was he who, in 1973, had made a Japanese translation of my book *The Text of the New Testament: Its Transmission, Corruption, and Restoration.*

I must mention yet another scholar whom I was happy to meet once again some forty years after he had been in the U.S.A. This was Toshio Hirunuma, who had come to study the Celtic languages under Joshua Whatmough at Harvard. As professor of classical and comparative philology at Kwansei Gakuin University, Dr. Hirunuma had over the years been most productive. Besides issuing a Greek-

Japanese lexicon of the New Testament, more recently he published several volumes in a Japanese series entitled The Praxis of New Testament Textual Studies. Since 1966 he had been issuing on a monthly basis successive installments of *Studia Textus Novi Testamenti,* which, as of March 1997, had reached page 2,768. Unhappily, because of the severe earthquake that struck Japan in 1994, Hirunuma's publications were temporarily interrupted when the printing house of Shalom was destroyed.

In 1990 an invitation came for me to lecture during the spring module of the academic calendar at the Caribbean Graduate School of Theology in Kingston, Jamaica. Its founding was sponsored interdenominationally in the eighties; the institution, under the supervision of Zenas Gerig, provides graduate education for theological students coming from a wide variety of Caribbean and Central American countries. The dean, Dieumème Noëlliste, was born in Haiti and earned his Ph.D. degree in the United States. My choice of subject for the accelerated module of three weeks was the exegesis of the Epistle to the Galatians, based on the Greek text. Although only a few students elected to take the course, I was gratified that they applied themselves diligently and, I think, eagerly.

My wife and I were housed comfortably in an apartment complex near the permanent residence of the Gerigs. Nearby stood a huge breadfruit tree. Neither my wife nor I had previously seen such a tree, which is native to Polynesia; the edible, round fruit has a texture like that of bread when baked or roasted.

The following year the president of the Seminario Internacional Teológico Bautista at Buenos Aires, Dr. Stanley Clark, invited me to teach two courses and offered to act as interpreter. Besides teaching at the seminary I was also invited to give a lecture in English at the Union Theological Seminary. On Sundays I was usually speaking, through an interpreter, to various congregations in the city. My wife, who is competent in Spanish, was a great help to me throughout our stay in Argentina.

In May of 1993 my wife and I returned to Korea, where I was to give a series of lectures on the book of Revelation to several hundred ordained elders of Presbyterian churches. We had accommodations at the elegant Lotte Hotel in Seoul, and the lectures were given in the newly constructed Korean Torch Mission Center. During the week of the lectures, Mr. Zeong-Duk Kim, president of a publishing house called Christianity Culture Association, issued a Korean translation of my book *The Canon of the New Testament.* I was happy to be presented with this during my visit.[10]

In 1996 I was invited to participate in an International Symposium on the Interpretation of the Bible held at Ljubljana, Slovenia, on the occasion of the publication of the first interconfessional Slovenian translation of the Bible. Sponsored by the Slovenian Academy of Sciences and Arts, in association with the Israel Academy of Sciences and Humanities, the Oriental Institute of Rome, and several other faculties and societies, the sessions brought together more than one hundred biblical scholars from many countries and cultures. Slovenia, the northwestern part of what had been Yugoslavia, is a little larger in area than Wales and a little smaller than New Jersey. According to the guidebook, "It is a nation of two million people with a distinctive and clear identity, which has preserved its individuality in this treacherous sub-alpine crossroads for 1,500 years, built and preserved during this period 3,000 churches, and created a rich artistic heritage."

The purpose of the symposium, organized by Professor of Theology Jože Krašovec, was twofold: to discuss the hermeneutic principles and the distinctive features of ancient and modern translations of the Bible, and to present the role of the Bible in Slavonic national cultures. The program also included an organ concert, an exhibition of

---

[10]In order to be able to publish the book while I was present in Korea, time for proofreading had been cut short, and the footnotes contain not a few mistakes in the spelling of Greek words.

Bibles organized by the National and University Library in Ljubljana, and the inauguration of the new translation of the Bible, the first to be prepared by both Roman Catholic and Protestant translators. I presented a paper on "The First Translation of the New Testament into Pennsylvania Dutch,"[11] which will be included in the volume of proceedings to be issued by the Slovenian Academy of Sciences and Arts. The ceremony of solemn inauguration of the interconfessional translation was opened with an address of welcome by Milan Kučan, president of the Republic of Slovenia, and was followed with brief comments made successively in Hebrew, Greek, English, German, French, Russian, Norwegian, and Slovene. I suppose that it was because of my being a trustee of the American Bible Society that I had been asked to make the English presentation.

---

[11] This translation, *Es Nei Teshtament,* was published in 1994 by the Bible League, South Holland, Illinois. The translators, Henry Hershberger and several other Amishmen, followed the procedures of the Wycliffe Bible translators.

Chapter 17

PRIZES, AWARDS, AND HONORS

APART from the prizes awarded me during my college and seminary days (mentioned in chapters 2 and 3), several others came my way in later years. Three of these were awarded by the Christian Research Foundation, the existence of which was brought to my attention in the early fifties by Professor Robert Pfeiffer of Harvard. It was during an afternoon break in our work of translating the books of the Apocrypha (see pp. 79–80 above) that Pfeiffer told us about a certain physician, Charles Griswold Campbell (1912–53), who had provided an endowment to establish the foundation. Several years earlier Dr. Campbell had asked Pfeiffer to read and assess the manuscript of a book he had written on "Race and Religion." The thesis of Campbell's book was that Jesus was not of Jewish decent but, like his mother, was a blond, blue-eyed Aryan type. The religion he taught rested, not on Old Testament antecedents, but on Zoroastrian teaching.

After reading the manuscript, Pfeiffer was inclined, he said, to tell Campbell bluntly that he thought it was "garbage." He decided, however, to take a less abrasive approach, and so he merely said that he himself held a different point of view from that expressed in the manuscript. Eventually, Dr. Campbell had his book printed in Holland and published, apparently at his own expense, through Peter Nevill, Ltd., in London.

Subsequently Dr. Campbell arranged through Pfeiffer and others at Harvard Divinity School for the incorporation of the Christian Research Foundation, the purpose of which was to sponsor annual competitions. The directors of the foundation were authorized to award each year up to three thousand dollars in prizes. Competition for the prizes was open to students and to writers in any country, but the papers submitted for consideration had to be written in English. Students who submitted entries were to enclose a letter of recommendation from their professor of New Testament or of church history. The committee selected by the foundation to read the essays would judge them for their historical acumen, originality, and stylistic distinction.

Pfeiffer suggested to me that one or more people at Princeton Seminary might well consider entering the competition. Accordingly, I advised a student of mine, Harold H. Oliver, to submit a copy of his Th.M. thesis entitled " 'Helps for Readers' in Greek New Testament Manuscripts," to the secretary of the foundation, Dr. Ralph Lazzaro of Harvard Divinity School. I also decided to submit a copy of my recently published book, *Annotated Bibliography of the Textual Criticism of the Testament.* Of the fifteen recipients of prizes awarded in the 1955–56 competition, Oliver and I each received five hundred dollars.

In subsequent annual competitions sponsored by the foundation nine other Princeton Seminary students who had written term papers or theses in New Testament were awarded prizes ranging from two hundred to seven hundred and fifty dollars. They were Norman A. Beck, James A. Brooks, Lawrence Eldridge, S. David Garber, John L. Kipp, John B. Mathews, Vernon Neufeld, Cullen Story, and Lawrence E. Yates. In 1962 and again in 1963 I was awarded one thousand dollars, having submitted the manuscripts of two books of mine, *Chapters in the History of New Testament Textual Criticism*[1] and *The Text of the New Testament.*

---

[1] Leiden: Brill, 1963.

Honorary Degrees

In previous years honorary degrees have aroused no little discussion in educational fields. For a time it was thought that some distinction should be made between a degree earned by a student and a degree conferred as an honor. As a compromise, only certain degrees are now awarded as honors. Honorary degrees are usually given to persons who have contributed to the arts or sciences or to the welfare of humanity. Sometimes, however, they have been given to prominent persons for the sake of publicity and for other less worthy reasons.

According to the *New Guinness Book of Records*,[2] the greatest number of honorary degrees awarded to any individual is 129, given to the Reverend Theodore M. Hesburgh, C.S.C. (born May 25, 1917), former president of the University of Notre Dame in Indiana.

Over the years a very great variety of degrees, honorary and earned, has been developed. Most readers will be surprised to learn that "more than 1,600 different academic degrees are currently conferred by colleges and universities in the United States. . . . In addition, more than 800 other academic degrees have been recognized in past years but, as far as can be determined, they are no longer in current use. Almost 2,600 different abbreviations are used for the 1,600 current degrees."[3]

---

[2]New York: Facts on File, 1994.

[3]Walter Crosby Eells and Harold A. Haswell, *Academic Degrees: Earned and Honorary Degrees Conferred by Institutions of Higher Education in the United States* (Detroit: Gale Research Co., 1970) 1. According to this handbook, the largest number of degrees is in engineering, about 350; then the field of education, more than 250; in business, more than 175; medical science, about 150. There are more than 250 "spurious" degrees, such as master of character analysis, diplomat of massotherapy, philosopher of metaphysics, philosopher of theology, doctor of divinity in bio-psycho-dynamic religions, doctor of spiritual divinity, and doctor of universal truth.

In 1951, sixteen years after I had been graduated from Lebanon Valley College with the A.B. degree, my alma mater bestowed on me the honorary degree of Doctor of Divinity (D.D.).

In 1962 the College (now University) of Findlay, Ohio, saw fit to confer on me the degree of Doctor of Humane Letters (L.H.D.).

In 1964 the University of St. Andrews, the third oldest university in the British Isles, honored me by conferring the Doctor of Divinity degree. It is the custom at St. Andrews on such occasions for the audience, made up chiefly of students, to begin clapping hands and stamping feet immediately following the reading of the laureation and not to cease until the recipient of the degree rises to acknowledge their demonstration.

In 1970 the University of Münster, at a special ceremony conducted after I had delivered a public lecture, conferred on me the honorary degree of Doktor der Theologie (D.Theol.) This was followed by a meal at a local restaurant, attended by members of the Faculty of Theology. The meal, called *Doktorschmaus,* was paid for in the following manner. Immediately following the convocation during which I presented the lecture (entitled "Namen für die Namenlosen in dem Neuen Testament"),[4] I was handed the honorarium for the lecture in German marks, and we proceeded at once to Hotel Schnellmann, where I played the host at the *Doktorschmaus,* making use of the German marks.

In 1985, during the six weeks of a lecture tour in South Africa, the University of Potchefstroom conferred on me the degree of Doctor Litterarum (D.Litt.) During the ceremony, held in the great hall so as to accommodate the parents and friends of those who were graduating, there

---

[4]An expanded form of the lecture under the title, "Names for the Nameless in the New Testament: A Study in the Growth of Christian Tradition," was published as a chapter in my book *New Testament Studies;* a summary appeared in *The Oxford Companion to the Bible.*

was a slight earthquake. The tremor was, however, so minor that I was unaware of it, and learned about it only at a later time.

Membership in Learned Societies

Besides having been a member of the Society of Biblical Literature and of the American Philological Association since my student days at Princeton, in 1950 I was the first American to be nominated for membership in the European-based Studiorum Novi Testamenti Societas (usually referred to as SNTS). This society, which first met at Birmingham in 1938, has an international membership, and at annual meetings papers are presented in English, German, and French. The meetings are held at a wide variety of academic institutions, and over the years I have been able to attend meetings held at Aarhus, Aberdeen, Bangor, Basel, Bonn, Cambridge, Canterbury, Edinburgh, Frankfurt, Göttingen, Gwatt, Heidelberg, Madrid, Milan, Newcastle,

Presidents of Studiorum Novi Testamenti Societas at the Jubilee meeting, Robinson College, Cambridge, 1988: R. H. Fuller, C. F. D. Moule, E. Lohse, W. D. Davies, C. K. Barrett, R. McL. Wilson, M. D. Hooker, B. M. Metzger, H. Greeven, E. Schweizer, M. de Jonge, R. E. Brown

Noordwijkerhout, Nottingham, Prague, Rome, St. Andrews, Strasbourg, Toronto, Trondheim, and Tübingen. The Jubilee meeting of the society was held in 1988 at Robinson College, Cambridge, when Professor Morna Hooker was president. A great many members attended this meeting, including eleven former presidents of the society.

In 1986 I was invited to become a member of the American Philosophical Society, a society organized in 1743 by Benjamin Franklin "for promoting useful knowledge." It supports and encourages scholarship in all fields of study. Its membership, which today is limited to about seven hundred, comprises scholars in the natural sciences, mathematics, philosophy, astronomy, and the humanities, as well as persons distinguished in music, jurisprudence, and the arts. The approximately 570 American members represent thirty states, and the 125 foreign members, about two dozen countries. Meetings are held twice a year at the society's headquarters in the historic section of Philadelphia, and accommodations and meals are provided by the society in local hotels. At these meetings, lasting two or three days, papers on a wide range of intellectual pursuits are read and discussed.

A most pleasant event was held in the spring of 1986 when members of the Philosophical Society were invited to attend the sessions of the general meeting of the Royal Society in London. The opening reception was held at the American Embassy and the closing banquet was served in the sumptuous quarters of Goldsmiths' Hall, near St. Paul's. The papers read at the joint sessions, published later in three volumes,[5] included two symposia: the Royal Society focussed on "Ethical Limits of Scientific Research," and the American Society on "Interactions of the Sciences and the Humanities."

An honor accorded few American scholars came to me in 1978 when I was elected corresponding fellow of the

---

[5] *Papers Read at a Joint Meeting of the Royal Society and the American Philosophical Society, April 1986* (Special Publication APS 44; Philadelphia: American Philosophical Society, 1987).

British Academy. Corresponding fellow is the Academy's highest distinction for persons who are not residents in the United Kingdom. Although I have not been able to attend many of the meetings, I made a special point to be present at the General Meeting held in July, 1994. On this occasion the F. C. Burkitt Medal for Biblical Studies was to be presented to me. This bronze medal, about two and three-quarter inches in diameter and three-sixteenths of an inch thick, bears on the obverse side the image of an open book resting on a mountain. On the right-hand page is the Latin text *vivvs est sermo Dei et efficax* ("The word of God is living and active," Hebrews 4:12), and around the upper half of the medal are the words *meos direxit gressvs* ("It [or, he] has directed my steps"). On the reverse side is a wreath within which are the words *fons sapientiae verbvm Dei* ("The word of God is a fountain of wisdom"). Incised on the edge of the medal is my name followed by the date, *mcmxciv*.

At the presentation of the medal the president of the Academy read the following citation:

> Through a long life of scholarly activity Professor Metzger has made a contribution to New Testament and related studies of unusual extent and value. In addition to many original and suggestive discussions of questions arising in the New Testament and elsewhere in ancient literature, he has written standard reference works on the Text of the New Testament, the Ancient Versions of the New Testament, and the Canon of the New Testament. He was one of the editors of the edition of the Greek New Testament now almost universally used. Very few living scholars have an equally wide and deep knowledge of the manuscript tradition of the biblical texts.

The award takes its name from Francis Crawford Burkitt, Norrisian Professor of Divinity in Cambridge University, who arranged to have medals struck for presentation annually by the British Academy to a scholar (whether a member of the Academy or not) in recognition of special service to biblical studies. Since 1925, when the medals began to be presented, three American scholars have been honored. The two earlier American scholars were James Hardy Ropes of Harvard Divinity School in 1928 and Joseph A. Fitzmyer, S.J., of Catholic University of America in 1984.

Over the past quarter of a century it has been my pleasant duty to serve as president of four learned societies. In August of 1971 at the Twenty-sixth General Meeting of Studiorum Novi Testamenti Societas, held at Leeuwenhorst Congress Center, Noordwijkerhout, The Netherlands, I presented my presidential address, entitled "Patristic Evidence and the Textual Criticism of the New Testament," later published in *New Testament Studies*.[6] At the business sessions of the society I made use of the gavel that a former student of mine, the Reverend Harlan H. Naylor, had kindly crafted for me from a block of walnut wood. He did this because I had casually mentioned to him, in connection with my forthcoming service as president, that previous business sessions of the society had been conducted sans gavel. After my tenure of office ended, I gave the gavel into the keeping of the secretary of the society, who has made it available to other presidents year-by-year.

In October of 1971 at the annual meeting of the Society of Biblical Literature, held in the Hyatt Regency House, Atlanta, Georgia, I delivered the presidential address, entitled "Literary Forgeries and Canonical Pseudepigrapha," later published in the *Journal of Biblical Literature*.[7]

In December of 1972 I served as president of the North American Patristic Society, meeting at Philadelphia in the Benjamin Franklin Hotel in conjunction with the annual meeting of its parent organization, the American Philological Association. Six papers were presented during the program but there was no presidential address. The custom of giving a presidential address began in 1981 with the first meeting that was independent of the American Philological Association.

---

[6]Volume 18 (1972) 379–400.
[7]Volume 91 (1972) 3–24.

The last occasion of my functioning in a presidential role was in April of 1995, at the Eighth International Interdisciplinary Conference of the Society for Textual Scholarship, held at the Graduate School and University Center of the City University of New York. This society, founded in 1979, is an organization devoted to interdisciplinary discussion of textual theory and practice. The society's members include scholars from many different fields, and a series of volumes, entitled *Text*,[8] contain articles selected from papers given at the biennial conferences, together with articles submitted independently. The subject of my presidential address was "Some Curious Bibles," in which I drew attention to a variety of oddities in printing and translation as well as unusual formats; it was published in volume 9 of the series.[9]

Other Honors

In 1955 Dr. Aziz S. Atiya, the director of the Higher Institute of Coptic Studies in Cairo, invited me to become an honorary member and corresponding fellow of the institute. Later, as organizing editor of the multivolume *Coptic Encyclopedia*,[10] Atiya asked me to contribute several articles, which I was happy to do.

In 1959 I was invited to become the American member of the Kuratorium of the Vetus Latina Institute, located at the Monastery of Beuron in Hohenzollern, on the upper Danube. Here, living in a self-contained environment, a succession of scholarly Benedictine monks had begun earlier in the century to collect evidence of the Old Latin text of the Bible preserved in patristic quotations. From 1949 onwards they published volumes of the Vetus Latina that

---

[8] *Text: Transactions of the Society for Textual Scholarship* (New York: AMS, 1984–).

[9] *Text: An Interdisciplinary Annal of Textual Studies* (Ann Arbor: The University of Michigan Press, 1996) 1–10.

[10] New York: Macmillan, 1991.

The Monastery of Beuron, located on the Donau (Danube)
where it cuts through a spur of the Schwabian Alps

are monuments of meticulous and accurate scholarship. On
two occasions I had the pleasure of visiting the monastery
and of making the acquaintance of the director of the
project, Bonifatius Fischer (a recipient of the Burkitt Medal
of the British Academy) and, later, the acquaintance his
successor, Hermann Josef Frede.

In 1961 I was elected a member of the advisory committee of the Institute for New Testament Textual Research
at Münster in West Germany. This committee, most of
whose members are Germans, also includes scholars in
Belgium, Britain, France, Greece, Holland, Israel, Italy, and
Luxemburg.

Earlier this century the custom arose among educational institutions in the United States to present special
citations to graduates of previous years who were deemed
to have made some noteworthy contribution. In accord
with this practice, in 1961 my alma mater, Lebanon Valley

Receiving a citation of appreciation at the 1990 Bible Week
luncheon of the Laymen's National Bible Association

College, presented me with its Distinguished Alumnus Award, a medallion inscribed with the words, "In recognition of distinguished achievement in the field of Biblical scholarship."

In 1989, five years after I had been retired from teaching, I received from Princeton Theological Seminary the Distinguished Alumnus Award in recognition of my work as chair of the New Revised Standard Version Bible Committee and in appreciation of a teaching career of forty-six years in the preparation of "countless seminary students, many of whom themselves became teachers." I had been, in fact, the dissertation supervisor of twenty-five doctoral candidates.

On November 16, 1990, the Laymen's National Bible Association, founded in 1940 and the sponsor of National Bible Week, celebrated the Fiftieth Annual National Bible Week at an interfaith luncheon held at the Plaza Hotel in New York City. Among the awards was a special presentation given to me as chair of the Standard Bible Committee "in recognition of outstanding service to the Bible cause."

Each of the more than three hundred guests at the luncheon received a copy of the recently published New Revised Standard Version of the Bible through the generosity of the six licensed publishers.

Festschriften

One of the ways in which colleagues and former students join in showing honor to an academic is by the presentation of a collection of essays. I have been the recipient of three such volumes. In 1981 the Clarendon Press at Oxford published a volume entitled *New Testament Textual Criticism: Its Significance for Exegesis: Essays in Honour of Bruce M. Metzger,* edited by Eldon J. Epp and Gordon D. Fee. The book, with a frontispiece of myself and a bibliography of my writings, contains twenty-nine contributions in English, French, and German, written by scholars from twelve different countries, including Russia and Japan.

Four years later, near the end of a lecture tour in South Africa and while at a dinner party at Potchefstroom, I was presented with a handsome handcrafted leather-bound volume containing the typescripts of twenty contributions, edited by J. H. Petzer and P. J. Hartin. The collection, entitled *A South African Perspective on the New Testament: Essays by South African New Testament Scholars Presented to Bruce Manning Metzger during His Visit to South Africa in 1985,* was published, with a frontispiece of myself and a supplementary bibliography of my writings, the following year by E. J. Brill of Leiden.

The third Festschrift, presented to me in typescript format at a surprise dinner party held in Princeton on my eightieth birthday in 1994, was edited by two of my former doctoral students, Bart D. Ehrman and Michael W. Holmes. Entitled *The Text of the New Testament in Contemporary Research: Essays on the* Status Quaestionis, the volume contains twenty-two contributions, many of them by younger scholars who have specialized in textual criticism. As it happens, the published form of the Festschrift appeared in 1995 as volume 46 in the series, Studies and Documents.[11] This is the same series in which, forty years earlier, my *Annotated Bibliography of the Textual Criticism of the New Testament* had been issued as volume 16.

A Portrait

One other honor still to be mentioned was particularly gratifying to me. This was the totally unexpected arrangement made to have my portrait painted. It came about in the following manner. In 1987, three years after my retirement from teaching at the Seminary, I was invited to give a series of lectures on the Sermon on the Mount at the Independent Presbyterian Church (U.S.A.) of Birmingham, Alabama, whose pastor, Dr. M. Scott McClure, had been graduated from Princeton Seminary in 1951. A year or two after delivering the lectures I was greatly surprised to learn that at his suggestion the church had decided to commission the painting of my portrait.

It was still more gratifying that the portrait was painted by another alumnus of the Seminary, David A. Walter, of the class of 1970, who had become associate dean of admissions at Swarthmore College in Pennsylvania and one of Philadelphia's leading portrait painters. After a number of sittings the work was finished and the portrait was hung in the main reading room of the seminary library. More than one person has told me that they think the painter produced a good likeness of me.

---

[11] Grand Rapids, Mich.: Eerdmans, 1995. A supplementary bibliography of my writings is included in an article entitled "Bruce Metzger as Textual Critic," by James A. Brooks in *The Princeton Seminary Bulletin,* New Series 15 (2, 1994) 156–64.

Chapter 18

INTERESTING PEOPLE I HAVE KNOWN

T HE title of this chapter must not be taken to imply that persons mentioned in previous pages were not inter-esting; it is only that I found it difficult to fit the following into the framework of the other chapters.

Alexander Haggerty Krappe

In the mid-forties my wife and I entertained at Sunday evening supper a savant who had recently moved to Prince-ton and whom I had met while he was doing research in the seminary library. His name, Alexander Haggerty Krappe, I recognized as being that of the translator of Robert Eisler's learned and controversial work, *The Messiah Jesus and John the Baptist.*[1]

After earning the Ph.D. degree in 1919 in the Depart-ment of Romance Languages and Literatures at the Univer-sity of Chicago, Krappe spent several years reading widely in the field of folklore and mythology in the British Mu-seum, the Bibliothèque nationale, and the Library of Con-gress. His publications included *Balor with the Evil Eye: Studies in Celtic and French Literature; The Legend of Roderick, Last of the Visigoth Kings, and the Ermanarich Cycle; Etudes de mythologie et de folklore germaniques; La leggenda di S. Eusta-chio; The Science of Folk-Lore; Mythologie universelle; La genèse*

---

[1]London: Methuen, 1931.

des mythes;[2] as well as scores of learned articles in a wide variety of journals and Festschriften.

When Krappe moved to Princeton in the early forties he brought with him a stack of filing drawers that extended from the floor to the ceiling of his apartment and that contained, he informed me, some two million slips of paper on which he had collected data through his wide reading over the years.

What interested me, however, was Krappe's editorial work in translating and condensing the nearly 1,500 pages of the German text of Eisler's two volumes entitled ΙΗΣΟΥΣ ΒΑΣΙΛΕΥΣ ΟΥ ΒΑΣΙΛΕΥΣΑΣ[3] (Jesus, a king who did not reign), a work characterized by F. F. Bruce as "a monument of misplaced ingenuity, and yet a repository of miscellaneous learning for the reader who can distinguish fact from theory."[4]

According to Eisler, there once existed a rich fund of historical tradition about Jesus among Jews and non-Christian Greeks and Romans. Almost all of this material had been deliberately destroyed, or falsified, by a system of rigid censorship officially authorized ever since the time of Constantine and reinstituted in the reigns of Theodosius II and Valerian III (AD 477). The chief pieces that escaped the censors, according to Eisler, are a score of passages preserved in the Old Russian version of Josephus's *Jewish War* that deal with the history of John the Baptist, Jesus, and the earliest disciples of Christ. On the basis of these passages, along with a variety of other Jewish and Christian sources, Eisler was able to portray Jesus as a political radical who was finally executed by the Romans for sedition.

---

[2]New York: Institut des études françaises, 1927; Heidelberg: C. Winter, 1923; Paris: E. Leroux, 1928; Aquila: Officine grafiche vecchioni, 1928; London: Methuen, 1930; Paris: Payot, 1930; Paris: Payot, 1938.

[3]Heidelberg: C. Winter, 1929–30. For the English edition, see n. 1 above.

[4]*In Retrospect: Remembrance of Things Past* (Grand Rapids: Eerdmans, 1980) 135.

Among several side issues that Krappe as editor decided to highlight, and in some cases to elaborate, is a discussion of Jesus' personal appearance. By adroit conjectural emendations, the adulatory description of Jesus in the well-known medieval *Letter of Lentulus* is made to describe Jesus as a crooked hunchback, only four feet seven inches in height, of terrible appearance, which struck all who approached him with horror.

Another of Krappe's interests was tracking down the curious tradition, which crops up in stray corners, that Jesus had a twin brother named Thomas—a subject that J. Rendel Harris had briefly explored in his book *The Twelve Apostles.*[5] An early text that contains several allusions to Jesus' twinship is *The Acts of Thomas,* extant in Greek and Syriac. Some months following my first acquaintance with Krappe, he asked me to translate for him the several passages in the Syriac version that refer to Thomas's twin brother. In view, however, of the availability of William Wright's accurate English translation of the treatise, I saw no need to provide a duplicate rendering of those passages.

In 1947 Dr. Krappe died in his fifty-third year. I have sometimes wondered what ever became of his extensive index to folklore and mythology.

Brother Anthony, A Carmelite Hermit

My personal contacts with Anthony M. Opisso were irregular and infrequent. During the nearly quarter of a century that I have known him he has been a Carmelite hermit living in a shelter in the woods belonging to the Cistercian Abbey of Our Lady of Calvary in the province of New Brunswick, Canada.

Born in 1923 of Spanish parents residing in the Philippines, Opisso earned the M.D. degree at the University of Chicago and then began a medical practice in western Montana. Following his recovery from a severe illness,

[5]Cambridge: W. Heffer & Sons, 1927.

during which he had promised the Lord that he would do something for God if he lived, he gave up his medical practice, sold his house and land, and left to do volunteer work at isolated mission hospitals in East Africa. There he spent six years immersed in an active schedule of seeing patients from morning to night, operating, doing hospital rounds, and travelling by ambulance to outlying medical stations.

It was amid such a life of hyperactivity that Anthony Opisso heard the call to enter a life of contemplation and prayer. And so it was that, after finding someone to replace him at the mission hospital, he left Africa and became a hermit attached to an abbey under the supervision of the Trappist Fathers of Rogersville, New Brunswick, where, at the time of this writing (1997), he has been a hermit for thirty-three years.

The first of the several occasions (all of them unexpected and unannounced) when Brother Anthony came to see me at Princeton was in 1975. At this time he brought me a copy of his recently published book, *The Bread of God*,[6] which is described on the title page as written "By a Trappist Monk who Prayed for a Carmelite Hermit who Wrote." The dust jacket identifies the monk as Brother Alberic, a Trappist of an abbey in the eastern part of the United States, and the author as a hermit in an abbey in eastern Canada. The reason for his visit to Princeton was to request me to write a brief evaluation of the book. After reading the volume I was happy to draw up a paragraph or two in which I commended his careful work.

In an enthusiastic foreword to the book Professor J. Duncan M. Derrett of London calls *The Bread of God* a remarkable and highly individual work. "There are many works of critical scholarship on the market, and many works of piety, many commentaries, and many meditations. This work has something of all of these, and yet cannot be described faithfully as any one of them. . . . I have met nothing like it before."

---

[6]New York: Vantage, 1975.

Derrett continues as follows:

> An example is the commentary on Mt. 13:31, Lk. 13:19.
> "Took and sowed" amounts to much the same as "sowed."
> Few will think that semitic idiom (did Jesus utter his par-
> ables in Aramaic, or in Mishnaic Hebrew?) will make more
> out of "took and sowed" than a simple "sowed." Yet it is a
> fact that the compilers (and their anonymous and unknown
> specialist advisors and their churches) deliberately pre-
> ferred to read "took and sowed" instead of St. Mark's
> simple "sowed," and that proves that they saw something
> special in "took." If Brother Anthony does not say the last
> word on their reasons, he draws our attention to the fact
> that a reason has to be found.

A few years later Brother Anthony and I conferred
more than once when he was doing research at the library
of Princeton Seminary. On this visit he was able to consult
books not available through interlibrary loan to the abbey
from St. Paul's University in Ottawa.

Subsequently Brother Anthony twice came to Princeton in order to present me with a copy of a recently
published book, but both times I was elsewhere giving
lectures. In 1985, when I was in South Africa, he brought
The Secret Joy of Repentance and in 1990, when I was at
Lynchburg, Virginia, he brought *The Revelation of the Son of
Man.*[7] The latter book was issued under Anthony's pen
name, Levi Khamor (*khamor* is the transliteration of the
Hebrew word meaning "ass").

The last time I saw Brother Anthony was August 27,
1992, when he appeared at our door shortly before the
evening meal. My wife, of course, invited him to stay for
supper and to sign our guest book. He had driven in a
rented car from the home of his godson, Anthony J. Rowe
of Geneva, New York, in order to consult with me about
overcoming the difficulties he had been having in finding a
publisher for a huge manuscript entitled *The Book of Under-*

---

[7]Boston: St. Paul Editions, 1985; Petersham, Mass.: St. Bede's
Publications, 1989.

standing, on which he had worked for many years. This manuscript was an encyclopedic work, comprising a veritable thesaurus of information about the concept of wisdom, knowledge, and understanding as reflected in the Bible, the Dead Sea Scrolls, Philo, the Pseudepigrapha, Midrashim, the Talmuds, the Zohar, and a wide range of church fathers, as well as ancient Egyptian, Ugaritic, Babylonian, and Greek writings. The reader is led, step-by-step, to contemplate how to live the "good life" by fulfilling the purpose for which one has been created.

For several years Brother Anthony (with a copy of a supporting letter from me) had been approaching a wide variety of publishers, including Thomas Nelson, Abingdon, Michael Glazier, Zondervan, Eerdmans, Paulist, Crossroad, Alba House, and the Franciscan University Press. But in each case the response had been negative. I was not quite sure how much further help I could give him when he visited me, other than to tell him that I myself had received negative responses from twelve publishers before E. J. Brill, the thirteenth that I solicited, agreed to take on the series, New Testament Tools and Studies (see pp. 149–51 above).

At any rate, in 1994 *The Book of Understanding* was finally published—with the *nihil obstat* and *imprimatur* of Donat Chiasson, archbishop of Moncton, New Brunswick—by the BenYamin Press of Geneva, New York (the publisher's address was that of Brother Anthony's godson). The book, comprising some 540 pages, was prepared for publication on the computer by his godson's wife, Nancy. The volume represents eighteen years of searching and analysis of the implication of Solomon's admonition, "Get wisdom, and with all thy getting get understanding" (Proverbs 4:7).

Jakob Jónsson of Reykjavík

In September of 1970, while planning for my return from Great Britain, I decided to stop off in Iceland in order to see something of the country and to visit an acquaintance, Dr. Jakob Jónsson.

About the size of the state of Virginia, Iceland has been called the land of ice and fire, because volcanoes erupt and hot springs steam beside glaciers and ice caps. Residents of the island take pride in having had a republican form of government and a national assembly as early as the year 930. In the year 1000 at the Icelandic Assembly a law was passed making Iceland a Christian country. With a total population today of about 265,000 persons, it is said that there are more book shops and libraries in proportion to the number of inhabitants than in any other country.

I arranged to stay three nights in one of the residence halls of the University of Iceland, located at Reykjavík, a city of about 80,000 persons—almost one-third of the population of Iceland. One morning I joined about forty other tourists for a sightseeing bus tour. In the evening we returned, having travelled nearly two hundred miles past lava fields and several small geysers spurting hot water and steam. During the trip we stopped several times, once to walk along the edge of an inactive volcano, and another to walk in Thingvellis, the field where the first *Althing* (national assembly) of fifty-two members had been held more than a thousand years earlier. Another memorable sight shown to tourists was the spectacular Gullfoss waterfall.

In addition to seeing sights in Iceland I also wished to renew acquaintance with a New Testament scholar whom I had met several times at meetings of the Society of New Testament Studies. Following the general meeting of SNTS, held at Heidelberg in August 1969, about twenty members, some with their wives, travelled to Tel Aviv to begin a ten-day study tour of important sites in Israel. During the day-to-day activities of the tour all of us came to appreciate Dr. Jónsson's wide interests and keen wit. Despite an August heat that was quite unaccustomed for the visitors from Iceland, the Jónssons were altogether ready and willing to participate fully throughout the tour.

For several years Jónsson had been serving as the pastor of a large Lutheran church in Reykjavík. He was also well known in Iceland as a playwright, poet, and author of several novels. His doctorate in theology was gained on the basis of a dissertation entitled "Humour and Irony in the New Testament, Illuminated by Parallels in Talmud and Midrash." Published in Reykjavík in 1965, it was reissued in 1985 by E. J. Brill of Leiden, with a foreword by Krister Stendahl, bishop of Stockholm. The scholarly content of the book impressed me, and later, when I was planning the

Hallgrímskirka, Reykjavík, Iceland

scope and contents of *The Oxford Companion to the Bible,* I invited Jónsson to write the article for that volume on "Irony and Humor in the Bible." Unhappily, his death on June 17, 1989 meant that he did not live to see the article in print when the volume was published a few years later.

I have pleasant recollections of having been entertained at afternoon tea in Dr. and Mrs. Jónsson's home. Later he took me to visit his church, Hallgrímskirkja, a remarkable specimen of ecclesiastical architecture designed by the late Professor Gujðón Samúelsson, one of the pioneers of Icelandic architecture in the present century. The main motif is crystallized basalt, which is found widely in Iceland. It is the tallest church in Iceland, with an elevator that goes up to the ninth floor. More significant is the name of the church, which commemorates a seventeenth-century clergyman, Hallgrímur Pétursson, the author of a celebrated poetic work, a cycle of fifty *Hymns of the Passion,* first published in Iceland in 1666. The hymns, which describe Christ's sufferings with unequalled tenderness and grace, were destined to guide and mold the spirituality of Icelandic Christianity for generations to come.

After my return to Princeton Dr. Jónsson kindly sent me a copy of the English translation of Pétursson's *Hymns,* prepared by Arthur Charles Gook and published at Reykjavík in 1966 by Hallgrim's church on the tercentenary of their first publication. Mr. Gook, a member of the "Open Brethren" in England, came to Iceland in 1905, where he wrote and published a number of books, both in English and in Icelandic. Toward the close of his life (Gook died in 1959), he began the translation of the Passion Hymns into English, keeping as far as possible the metrical form of the original. I have more than once tried to interest publishers in North America to issue a reprint of the volume. Unhappily, however, thus far none has seen fit to do so.

I cherish my memory of Jakob Jónsson, a man whose energy and insights exerted an influence on all who knew him. He recognized that "for everything there is a season . . . a time to weep, and a time to laugh" (Ecclesiastes 3:1, 4).

In 1994 a memorial volume entitled *Biblían og bókmenntirnar,* with a picture of Dr. Jónsson as frontispiece, was issued in his honor as vol. 9 of *Studia Theologica Islandica.* I was happy to accept the editor's invitation to join other friends of Dr. Jónsson in expressing through a brief article my appreciation for the life and work of a gifted and versatile scholar and churchman.

Charles C. Austin and His "Christian Bible"

Among curious editions of the Bible is the so-called *Christian Bible,* compiled and edited by Carl C. Austin and printed at his own expense in 1978 by Century Printing Co., Raleigh, North Carolina. The title page indicates that this is an "Integrated Version, Interpreted Edition, based on the King James Version with corrected translation from the Greek reinterpreted in the light of these corrections; including several newly recognized Testaments not previously authenticated; each passage comprehensively explained and cross-referenced."

Mr. Austin was born in New Jersey and grew up on a farm near Philadelphia, Pennsylvania. He attended Princeton University in the early 1930s, when his formal education was interrupted by the Depression.[8] His first job during those days of economic upheaval was that of a seaman on a freighter. Austin later entered the field of business management and worked for many years as a problem solver, conducting seminars in various parts of the United States and overseas with the U.S. State Department. He served as director of international management groups. In later life, as an Episcopalian layman, he was inducted into the Order of St. Luke, an interdenominational healing ministry.

---

[8]The information contained in this paragraph was supplied by Austin to the column "Church News" in the May 27, 1981, issue of the local newspaper of Whispering Pines, North Carolina, where he had resided since 1977.

On several occasions Austin wrote to me concerning his plan to prepare a special edition of the Bible. As our correspondence continued I began to sense the direction in which his thinking was taking him. Finally, one spring at the time of class reunions at Princeton University, he came to see me and I had opportunity to discuss face-to-face certain features of his project that seemed to me ill-advised or totally wrong. He remained convinced, however, that he had a valid, if unconventional, insight into the Christian Scriptures. We parted amicably, agreeing that different people have different views about the Bible.

Several years later I received through the mail a copy of *The Christian Bible,* a book of xvi + 657 pages, with gold edges and a leatherette black cover. The bulk of the volume presents the four Gospels woven together into forty-six chapters. These are followed by the three Epistles of John, the (apocryphal) *Epistles of Jesus and King Abgar of Edessa,* the Acts of the Apostles, the Epistles of Paul (including Hebrews but not Philemon), several of which are abbreviated, and portions of James, 1 and 2 Peter, and Jude. Instead of the book of Revelation, Austin's Bible concludes with a short section of *The Shepherd of Hermas,* and the fragmentary *Gospel of Peter.* About 150 pages follow presenting nine appendixes, the longest of which "corrects" 340 errors in the four Gospels and 1 John.

It will be noticed that no part of the Old Testament is included in the volume. Furthermore, statements in the New Testament that may be taken to authenticate the Old Testament are declared to be substandard or outright erroneous. For example, in introducing the Epistle to the Hebrews Austin declares:

> This Epistle is not of any use and is actually of negative value to the Christian faith in teaching it. The few statements in it concerning Jesus which are true are so heavily outweighed by the voluminous misconceptions and false statements, it offers in fact a Jewish interpretation of Jesus' ministry which makes it appear that Jesus was a product of Jehovah and the Old Testament, which he surely was

not. . . . This Epistle should therefore never be included in any New Testament used for teaching purposes or religious services in Jesus' name. The reason Paul colored this Epistle in favor of the Jewish scriptures so heavily was undoubtedly in fear of cruel treatment had he done otherwise. (p. 464)

The section of Galatians 3:16–18 is entitled "Paul becomes confused as to the origin of Jesus." Austin comments as follows:

In this passage and the verses which follow, Paul mistakenly assumes that Jesus was, as so many claimed in those days, "of the seed of Abraham," and a beneficiary of the promises made to Abraham by Jehovah. That this is not true is attested to by Jesus in John 8:33–40. . . . It is evident therefore that Paul was seeking to ingratiate himself with the Jews by aligning himself with them. (p. 447)

Several times Austin attempts to correct what he regards as mistranslations from the original Greek. For example, he argues that the unnamed "disciple whom Jesus loved" is not John but is Mary Magdalene. Consequently, the King James translation of John 13:23–25 is modified so as to read as follows: "Now there was leaning on Jesus' bosom one of his disciples, whom Jesus loved. Simon Peter therefore beckoned to her, that she should ask who it should be of whom he spoke. She then lying on Jesus' breast saith unto him, 'Lord, who is it?' " In the comment following these verses Austin declares:

There has been much discussion as to who this disciple was who was lying on Jesus' breast, but it can be said without question to have been Mary Magdalene. This confusion was caused by the fact that the Greek pronoun has no gender,[9] and translators have consistently assumed that a disciple had to be a man. Therefore "her" and "She" were mistakenly translated as "him" and "He" in this passage and elsewhere.

---

[9]Austin overlooks the fact that the gender of the third person singular pronouns in Greek (as also in Aramaic) is clearly distinguished.

Other explanations of the text, based on what Austin calls "odic connections which enable thought transference from one person to another over great distances" (p. 19), are arbitrary and strikingly eccentric. In comments on the healing of the nobleman's son (John 4:46–54), one reads,

> When Jesus asked his Father in heaven to heal the boy if it was wise for him to be well, his Father mentally visited the boy's mind and told it to heal his body. A fever is the spirit world's way of evicting any alien hostile spirit who has caused such an illness, making it too uncomfortable to remain. This is why fever breaks so quickly once such has been cast out. (p. 68)

About ten years after *The Christian Bible* had been printed, I was surprised to receive a letter from a legal firm in North Carolina stating that Austin had died September 16, 1987, and had bequeathed to me the remaining copies of *The Christian Bible.* Before I had opportunity to respond stating that I did not want the copies, the Theological Book Agency informed me that a shipment of about 1,200 copies had arrived and that I should make arrangements to pick them up.

It goes without saying that I was nonplussed; I had no wish to accept the shipment nor did I think that the copies would benefit anyone else. So I did nothing. Eventually, since the books were taking up space needed for other purposes, the director of facilities at the Seminary had them recycled.

Postscript

ACCORDING to an ancient Chinese proverb, "The faintest ink is more lasting than the strongest memory." Over the years it has been my practice, when reading books and articles, to enter on three-by-five-inch slips of paper bibliographical references, ideas, and comments that struck me as particularly noteworthy. Now numbering nearly twenty thousand, these slips are arranged alphabetically in file drawers[1] according to topics, catch words, and scriptural references. From scores of slips that are identified as "bon mot," the following have been selected as specimens.

> The most valuable of all talents is that of never using two words when one will do.
> — THOMAS JEFFERSON

> Let courage teach you when to speak and tact teach you how.
> — LYMAN ABBOTT

> The difference between the right word and the almost right word is the difference between lightning and a lightning bug.
> — MARK TWAIN

> Time is the deposit each one has in the bank of God, and no one knows the balance.
> — R. W. SOCKMAN

---

[1] The file drawers are eventually to be put in the archives of the library at Princeton Theological Seminary.

Mankind more frequently requires to be reminded than informed.

— SAMUEL JOHNSON

The best way to make your dreams come true is to wake up.

— PAUL VALÉRY

There is no right way to do the wrong thing.

— ANONYMOUS

You can't change the past, but you can ruin the present by worrying about the future.

— ANONYMOUS

We would never have heard about the Good Samaritan if he had only had good intentions.

— MARGARET THATCHER

Everything is what it is, and not another.

— BISHOP BUTLER

No one can make you feel inferior without your consent.

— ELEANOR ROOSEVELT

The church is the only society in the world that exists for the benefit of those who are not its members.

— WILLIAM TEMPLE

The test of good manners is the ability to put up with poor ones.

— ANONYMOUS

Some people love their own opinion, not because it is true, but because it is theirs.

— AUGUSTINE

We are not Christian because we do good works; we do good works because we are Christian.

— MARTIN LUTHER

Original sin is the only empirically verifiable Christian doctrine.

— RICHARD NEUHAUS

If you were arrested for being a Christian, would there be enough evidence to convict you?

— ANONYMOUS

I must continually remind myself as I lecture: if God is
God then it is ridiculous to talk about him as if he is
not present.

— Lesslie Newbigin

To say that God is love means that he either is or will become incarnate.

— George Santayana

God grant me the serenity
To accept the things I cannot change,
The courage to change the things I can,
And the wisdom to know the difference.

— Friedrich Christoph Oetinger

It is more important to speak about the Christ of our experience than our experience of Christ.

— James B. Torrance

It is meaningful to talk about God's eye without inquiring
about its color.

— Wolf-Dieter Just

God instituted prayer in order to lend his creatures the dig-
nity of causality.

— Blaise Pascal

Work will be prayer only if there is also prayer which is
not work.

— E. J. Yarnold, S.J.

Life must be lived forwards, but can only be understood
backwards.

— Søren Kierkegaard

INDEX